D0370062

Tapas and Appetizers

BY JOSE SARRAU

Translated by Francesca Piemonte Slesinger

A FIRESIDE BOOK

Published by Simon & Schuster Inc.
New York

A Fireside Book
Published by Simon & Schuster, Inc.
Simon & Schuster Building
Rockefeller Center
1230 Avenue of the Americas
New York, New York 10020

Originally published in Spain as *Tapas y Aperitivos* by Ediciones Sarrau in
the Spanish Language, © 1975 by Jose Sarrau
FIRESIDE and colophon are registered trademarks of
Simon & Schuster, Inc.

Designed by Irving Perkins Associates
Manufactured in the United States of America
1 2 3 4 5 6 7 8 9 10
Library of Congress Cataloging in Publication Data
Sarrau, Jose.
    Tapas and appetizers.

    Translation of: Tapas y aperitivos.
    "A Fireside book."
    1. Cookery (Appetizers)   2. Cookery, Spanish.
I. Title.   II. Title: Tapas and appetizers.
TX740.S31413   1987   641.8'12   86-33724
ISBN: 0-671-62555-1

Acknowledgments

We would like to gratefully acknowledge the work of Sr. Quintanilla, *Dibujante a plumilla*, creator of the original illustrations for *Tapas y Aperitivos*, some of which appear herein.

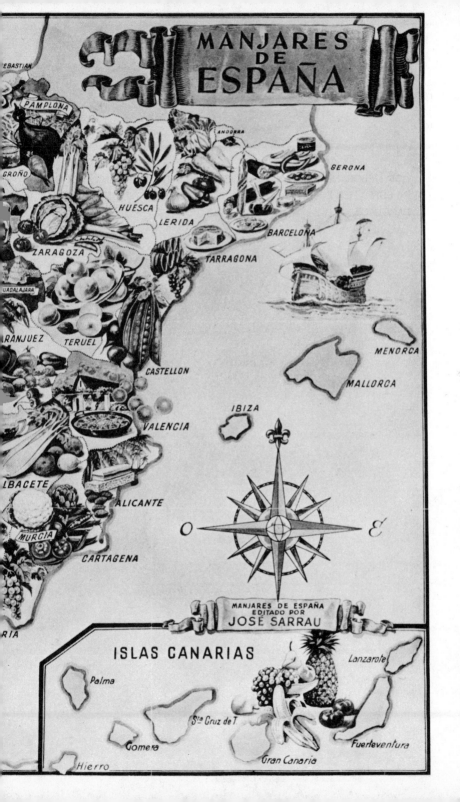

FOR DEBORAH BERGMAN, WHO DISCOVERED THIS BOOK IN SPAIN AND INVESTED HER ENERGY AND VISION INTO BRINGING IT TO THE ENGLISH LANGUAGE.

Contents

Contents

About Tapas

For anyone who has ever visited or lived in Spain, few traditions leave a more vivid memory than that of sharing tapas and a drink with friends. *Tapas*, or "little plates of little things," as Jose Sarrau calls them, are tiny morsels of food savored before lunch or dinner with a glass of dry sherry, wine, or frothy beer. In Spain, most bars, taverns, and special tapas restaurants called *colmados* pride themselves on their own unique tapas spreads, which can include anything from an onion and olive tart to spicy grilled shrimp in garlic sauce, but almost always include simple and delicious favorites like the potato and onion Spanish tortilla, and creamy croquettes. More than just a delicious snack, tapas celebrate the spontaneity, color, and spice of Spain and its people by melding

the most delectable aspects of food and friendship into a single national pastime.

Coming from the Spanish verb *tapar*, "to cover," it is said that tapas originated with the common practice in drinking establishments of placing a small dish of food on top of a drink. Often salty, this "tapa" encouraged the customer to drink more. Today, an offering of little dishes of marinated mushrooms, skewered seafood, or cold potato omelette presented on the countertops of Spanish bars and taverns is an almost requisite accompaniment to any drink. As Mary Hillgarth put it:

> The whole rhythm of life in Spain among the rich was Edwardian until 1936, and even now late hours are common everywhere, so it is not surprising that Spain has invented the *tapa*. Even in England, with some sort of tea between meals, people snatch eagerly at the leathery potato chips and tired biscuits their hosts or wives *may* provide with the gin or whiskey. The same applies to the pre-lunch drinks and, since breakfast in Spain is a sketchy affair of coffee and toast, every hostess worthy of the name produces delectable accompaniments to aperitifs such as sherry or martini (vermouth).

Visitors to Spain find the tapas ritual an easy and delicious way to participate in Spanish culture. Even during a short visit, it's easy to acquire favorite *tascas*, or tapas bars, with their various specialities. Frequented by grandmothers, students, and business people alike, any establishment that serves tapas is a place for everyone. So convenient and abundant are they that it is difficult to walk past their open doors without at least a glimpse or sniff of the daily offering. Few Spaniards actually *think* about stopping

for a tapa or two—they simply do so, coat, briefcase, purse, or books in hand.

In recent years, and to no one's surprise, food establishments serving tapas have appeared in several large cities in the United States. Due to the demands of the North American business day, the sharing of tapas with friends in this country is likely to be restricted to the late afternoon or early evening hours, and we may see an increasing number of urban restaurants or cafés serving "happy hour" drinks along with tender rings of fried squid or a codfish croquette or two. But tapas, as a culinary tradition lovingly nurtured in gatherings of friends, is a wonderful and versatile way of entertaining a group of any size at home.

Jose Sarrau worries that long lines and crowds at some of the most popular tapas bars in Spain may rob the tapas tradition of its spontaneity and intimacy. Nonetheless, and perhaps as a way of preserving a legacy which for decades has led many foreigners back to Spain in search of the best tapas, Sarrau now gives American cooks the secrets to keeping the tradition alive at home in this first English edition of his classic collection of tapas recipes. Spanish restaurateurs and home cooks have had this collection on their shelves for a number of years. Quick and easy to prepare, the recipes in this book, which come from all over the Iberian peninsula itself, and even include a few dishes from the Canary Islands, can be served either as an assortment of finger food or, for a more formal and festive occasion, as the centerpiece of a main meal.

There is no secret—other than practice and imagination—to re-creating tapas in the American kitchen. As with any cooking style, the freshest ingredients make the best tapa, and although some basic ingredients are difficult to find in the United States, good substitutes can be used. The Glossary on page 179 describes ingredients and utensils typically used in Spanish cooking, lists equivalents and substitutes readily available in supermarkets or specialty shops in this country, as well as explaining some simple techniques and basic recipes used in this book.

Whatever the site of your gathering, select tapas recipes that complement each other—perhaps one fried seafood dish, some flaky pastries filled with cheese, and spicy marinated mushrooms. Also, keep in mind how much time is available to prepare the tapas. Many can be made in advance with little or no last-minute preparation. Others require very little work, but must be prepared within minutes of serving.

For a small last-minute get-together with friends, this book offers some suggestions for even the humblest of foods commonly found in a kitchen: a piece of cheese, lightly brushed with olive oil and then grilled and served on a small piece of crusty bread, is no less a tapa than the noblest dish of mussels, crab, and shrimp in saffron rice!

Whether the tapas are simple items that can be prepared in seconds or more elaborate dishes that require planning, the recipes in this book offer a variety of delicious and often unusual treats that will enliven any party with the zest, friendliness, and flavors of Spain.

—Francesca Piemonte Slesinger

FRIED ALMONDS

TOASTED ALMONDS

TOASTED PEANUTS

TOASTED PINE NUTS WITH RAISINS

WALNUT, FIG, AND TOAST MIX

TUNA CROQUETTES (COD CROQUETTES, EGG CROQUETTES)

TUNA AND CHEESE CROQUETTES WRAPPED IN RICE

SHRIMP CROQUETTES

LITTLE SHRIMP AND CHEESE BALLS

BEEF CROQUETTES

1.

TOASTED NUTS, CROQUETTES, AND BANDERILLAS:
An Assortment of the Simplest Finger Foods

PICADOR'S CROQUETTES

FRIED BANDERILLA ASSORTMENT

CHICKEN BREAST PINCHOS WITH FOIE GRAS

"RASTRO" SANDWICHES

PINCHOS SARRAU

CHORIZO AND ONION PINCHOS

SPICY MINTY LAMB KEBOBS

ROAST PORK PINCHOS

MUSSEL AND CURED HAM PINCHOS

Tapas do not have to be complicated to be good. The next few pages contain some of the simplest tapa recipes, easy to prepare and eat. Made with readily available ingredients, they are perfect fare for an impromptu gathering.

In Spain's tapas bars, golden toasted or lightly sautéed nuts are served with the finest sherries and wines. The nuts are fried lightly in a little oil or roasted in the oven until browned, a seemingly simple step, but just enough to lend a Mediterranean flavor to a common American snack. Almonds and pine nuts are two nut varieties found in abundance in the Mediterranean. They make a delicious and nutritious snack when served with raisins, or figs and toast as suggested in the following recipes. Served by the handful or ground and added to sauces, nuts are a cherished staple in Spanish cooking, and the classic accompaniment to a glass of dry sherry. Preparation and cooking time vary with each variety, and all the variations are listed here.

Croquettes are tiny balls of minced meat, seafood, or cheese that are mixed with a rich white sauce, coated with an egg batter, rolled in bread crumbs, and fried until golden. Quite common among the daily offerings in Spain's tapas bars, they are often found on the dinner table as well.

The more traditional tuna, codfish, beef, and cheese croquettes are an imaginative and festive way to use leftovers, prepared with white sauce, as are some unusual variations—a mashed potato and pimento croquette, and tuna and cheese croquettes blanketed in white rice, then fried until golden. Croquettes can be made with almost any meat, fish, or cheese as a base, and prepared in advance up to the point of frying. Served warm and slightly crispy on the outside, croquettes are quite light and moist, yet filling enough to appease even the largest of appetites until dinner. Try them with fresh squeezed lemon, or hot sauce.

What could be more appetizing than medleys of salty olives, fresh cheeses, plump shellfish, and sizzling sausages, all colorfully arranged on tiny sticks—a treat for the eye as well as the palate. *Banderillas* (also known as *pinchos*) are scrumptious and colorful tidbits of food threaded onto a toothpick or tiny skewer and served with a cold drink.

Banderillas offer something for everyone. They can be prepared at whim, using whatever you find in the refrigerator, as well as in the combinations suggested in the next few pages. If you're serving a crowd, banderillas can be assembled in advance and served raw, or they can be broiled or fried at the last minute, if that's what the recipe calls for. What's more, they are held easily with one hand, which makes them a natural menu choice for a cocktail party or informal dinner.

FRIED ALMONDS
ALMENDRAS FRITAS

SERVES 8

½ pound shelled almonds
oil for frying
salt

1. Place the almonds in a saucepan, and add just enough water to cover. Bring to a boil and cook for 1 minute. Remove from heat. With a slotted spoon, remove the almonds from the saucepan, 10 to 12 at a time. Remove the loosened skins and place the peeled nuts in a bowl of cold water to cover. When all the almonds have been peeled and refreshed in the cold water, drain the water and reserve the nuts.

2. Pour the oil to ¼ inch deep in a large skillet and heat until hot but not sizzling. Fry the almonds one layer deep at a time, until golden. Remove from the skillet with a slotted spoon and drain on paper towels. Salt to taste and serve.

TOASTED ALMONDS
ALMENDRAS TOSTADAS

SERVES 8

½ pound shelled almonds
salt

1. The almonds may be toasted with or without skins. To blanch the almonds to remove the skins, see the recipe for Fried Almonds (page 17), step 1. After draining the almonds, salt to taste.

2. Heat the oven to 400°F. Spread the nuts on a cookie sheet in a single layer and place on the middle rack of the oven. Toast until golden. Let cool and serve.

or

1. To toast almonds in their skins, rinse under cold running water and drain in a colander. Add salt to taste. Let stand for 1 hour.

2. Heat the oven to 375°F. Spread the nuts on a cookie sheet in a single layer, and place on the middle rack in the oven. Toast for 20 to 30 minutes, or until the inside of one almond, when tested, is golden brown. Let cool and serve.

VARIATION: Toss the almonds with ¼ cup fine-quality olive oil to coat. Salt if desired.

TOASTED PEANUTS
CACAHUETES TOSTADOS (Alcahueses Torraos)

SERVES 8

½ pound shelled peanuts, or ¾ pound unshelled
salt

1. For unshelled peanuts, rinse the peanuts under cold running water in a colander. Drain and salt if desired.

2. Preheat the oven to 350°F. Spread the peanuts in a single layer on a cookie sheet and place on the middle rack in the oven. Toast for 20 to 30 minutes, or until the shells are completely dry and slightly browned and the peanut inside is golden and toasted through.

or

1. For shelled peanuts (panchitos), preheat the oven to 350°F. Spread the nuts in a single layer on a cookie sheet. Place the sheet on the middle rack in the oven and toast until the skins can be easily removed, about 20 to 30 minutes.

2. Remove the nuts from the oven and empty them into a dish towel or other soft cloth. Rub the nuts through the towel until the skins are completely removed. Salt to taste. Let cool and serve. For a saltier taste, first soak the shelled nuts in salted water to cover for 1 hour, drain well, and follow the same preparation for toasting as for unshelled peanuts.

TOASTED PINE NUTS WITH RAISINS
PIÑONES TOSTADOS

SERVES 6 TO 8

2 cups pine nuts
salt (optional)
2 cups seedless raisins

1. Place the pine nuts in a colander and rinse under running water. Drain well. Season the nuts with salt if desired.

2. Preheat the oven to 375°F. Spread the pine nuts in a single layer on a cookie sheet, and place on the middle rack of the oven. Bake until lightly toasted, about 5 to 7 minutes. Watch the nuts carefully to prevent burning.

3. Add the seedless raisins to the toasted nuts, mix well, and serve.

WALNUT, FIG, AND TOAST MIX
NUECES, HIGOS, Y PAN

Simple but delicious!

SERVES 6 to 8

1 cup day-old bread cubes
3 tablespoons butter, melted
1 cup chopped dried figs
1 cup toasted or plain walnut halves

1. Preheat the oven to 350°F.

2. Place the bread cubes in a bowl. Melt the butter in a saucepan and drizzle over the bread cubes, tossing to coat. Spread the cubes on a cookie sheet, and bake until lightly toasted.

3. Combine the toasted bread, figs, and walnut halves in a bowl, and mix well.

TUNA CROQUETTES (Cod Croquettes, Egg Croquettes)
CROQUETAS DE ATUN

This version of the venerable tuna croquette, a favorite tapa all over Spain, is crisp and golden on the outside, moist and melting on the inside. Surprisingly delicate in both taste and texture, it's likely to become a favorite finger food in your home. All croquettes can be prepared to the point of frying up to 24 hours in advance.

MAKES ABOUT 24

6 tablespoons lard or vegetable oil
1 heaping tablespoon finely chopped onion
⅔ cup all-purpose flour, plus extra for dredging
2 cups hot milk
1 6½-ounce can albacore or chunk light tuna, drained and
    flaked
salt and freshly ground black pepper to taste

pinch grated nutmeg
2 eggs, slightly beaten
1 cup fresh bread crumbs
oil for frying

1. Heat the 6 tablespoons lard or vegetable oil in a small sauce-pan over low heat. Add the onion, and sauté until transparent but not browned. Gradually add the flour, stirring to form a smooth paste. Whisk in the milk, and continue to cook, stirring constantly, until the mixture begins to thicken. Add the tuna, and season with the salt, pepper, and nutmeg. Cook for 1 to 2 minutes longer. Remove from heat and let cool.

2. Cover a large plate with flour for dredging. Scoop up tea-spoonfuls of the tuna mixture, and form bite-size oval shapes. Roll the croquettes in the flour, dip them in the egg, and roll them in the bread crumbs. Set aside.

3. Pour oil in a large skillet or deep-fryer to ½ inch deep, and heat until hot but not sizzling. Quickly fry the tuna croquettes until golden, turning once. Remove with a slotted spoon, and drain on paper towels. Serve hot.

VARIATIONS: For cod croquettes, substitute ½ pound poached, flaked codfish for the tuna.

For egg croquettes, substitute 4 to 6 chopped hard-boiled eggs and 1 to 2 teaspoons concentrated beef broth.

TUNA AND CHEESE CROQUETTES WRAPPED IN RICE
CROQUETAS DE ATUN CON QUESO

A light, multilayered, multiflavored treat. In this variation on the traditional croquette the filling is a flavorful blend of tuna and cheese mixed with egg yolk instead of bechamel.

MAKES ABOUT 15

2 ounces fresh cheese (farmer cheese, feta, or other preferred soft white fresh cheese)
1 3½-ounce can albacore or chunk light tuna, drained and flaked
¼ cup finely chopped fresh parsley
3 egg yolks, plus 1 slightly beaten egg
salt and freshly ground black pepper
1 cup cooked rice
4 tablespoons grated cheese (Gruyère, Parmesan, Cheddar, or other preferred melting cheese)
oil for frying
½ cup fresh bread crumbs

1. Mix the fresh cheese, tuna, parsley, and 1 egg yolk in a bowl until blended. Add salt and pepper to taste. Scoop up bite-size portions (about 15) of the mixture, and roll into balls. Set aside.

2. In a separate bowl, mix together the rice, the remaining 2 egg yolks, and the grated cheese, forming a paste. Place 1 tablespoon of the rice mixture in the palm of one hand, then place one tuna-cheese ball in the center of the rice mixture. Pack the rice around the tuna ball, patting it well to coat the tuna ball completely and evenly. The croquettes can be prepared up until this point and refrigerated until you are ready to serve them.

3. Pour the oil into a large skillet to ½ inch deep, and heat. Dip the tuna balls in the slightly beaten egg, then roll in the bread crumbs to cover. Fry the balls in the hot oil until golden. Drain on paper towels, and serve hot.

SHRIMP CROQUETTES
CROQUETAS DE MARISCOS

Shrimp croquettes are especially delicious with chilled white wine or a dry, fruity sherry such as manzanilla.

MAKES ABOUT 24

¾ pound raw shrimp, steamed, shelled, and deveined
3 tablespoons butter or olive oil
1½ tablespoons finely diced cooked ham, or 1 heaping teaspoon finely chopped onion
¼ cup all-purpose flour, plus extra for dredging
1 cup hot milk
pinch grated nutmeg
salt and freshly ground pepper to taste
2 eggs, slightly beaten
1 cup fresh bread crumbs
oil for frying

1. Chop the shrimp, and set aside.

2. Melt the butter or oil in a saucepan over low heat. Add the ham or onion. Stir in the ¼ cup flour, blending well and taking care not to brown. Slowly whisk in the milk and bring to a boil, whisking constantly, until the mixture is thickened. Add the shrimp and seasonings. Simmer for 1 minute longer, stirring constantly, and remove from heat. Pour the mixture into a bowl, and set aside to cool completely.

3. Scoop up heaping teaspoonsful of the shrimp mixture to form bite-size balls or oval shapes. Roll each ball lightly in the remaining flour, dip in the egg to coat, then roll in the bread crumbs. Set aside on a plate.

4. Pour oil for frying into a large skillet to ½ inch deep and heat until hot but not sizzling (or use a deep fryer). Fry the croquettes in the hot oil until golden. Remove with a slotted spoon, and drain on paper towels. Serve hot.

LITTLE SHRIMP AND CHEESE BALLS
BOLITAS DE CHESTER

Fry these rich yet light morsels and watch their grated cheese coating sizzle to a golden crust. Bite into one, and savor the subtle custardy filling flecked pink and white with shrimp. A relatively easy preparation yields a close to spectacular effect.

MAKES ABOUT 24

3 tablespoons butter
1 teaspoon minced shallot
¼ cup all-purpose flour, plus extra for dredging
1 cup hot milk
¼ pound shelled and deveined shrimp, finely chopped (see Note)
½ pound grated English Cheshire, Manchego, Gruyère, or other mild hard cheese
salt and freshly ground white pepper
pinch grated nutmeg
vegetable oil for frying
1 egg, slightly beaten

1. Melt the butter in a saucepan over low heat. Add the shallot, and sauté for 1 minute. Gradually add ¼ cup flour, stirring constantly to form a paste. Whisk in the milk and cook and stir until the mixture is thick and smooth. Add the shrimp, and simmer for 1 minute longer.

2. Remove from heat. Stir in 4 tablespoons of the cheese. Season with salt, pepper, and nutmeg to taste. Set the mixture aside until cool enough to handle, 30 to 45 minutes.

3. Scoop up heaping teaspoonsful of the cheese mixture and roll into bite-size balls. Roll the balls in flour and let cool completely for 20 to 30 minutes in the refrigerator or 30 to 45 minutes at room temperature.

4. Pour oil into a large skillet to ½ inch deep and heat until hot but not sizzling. While oil is heating, dip the cheese balls in the egg yolk and roll in the remaining grated cheese. Quickly fry the balls until golden. Drain on paper towels, and serve hot.

NOTE: An equal quantity of any other shellfish or foie gras may be substituted for the shrimp.

BEEF CROQUETTES
CROQUETAS DE CARNE

A felicitous use for leftover meat.

MAKES ABOUT 36

olive or vegetable oil for frying
2 heaping teaspoons finely chopped onion
¾ cup all-purpose flour
2 cups hot milk
salt and freshly ground black pepper to taste
pinch nutmeg
10 ounces cooked beef, such as stewed beef shank or pot roast,
   shredded into small bits
2 eggs, slightly beaten
2 cups fresh bread crumbs

1. Heat the ⅓ cup oil in a large saucepan. Add the onion, and sauté until transparent. Whisk in the flour, blending well. Stir in the milk, a little at a time, whisking well after each addition. Add the seasonings and cook for 1 minute longer, stirring constantly. Stir in the meat, blending well. Remove from heat, and pour the sauce into a bowl. Dust the sauce lightly with flour, and let cool.

2. Scoop up bite-size portions of the mixture with a spoon. On a lightly floured surface, roll the portions into small balls or oval shapes. Dip the balls in the egg to coat, then roll them in the bread crumbs. Set aside.

3. Pour oil into a large skillet to about ½ inch deep, and heat. Fry the croquettes in the hot oil until golden. Remove with a slotted spoon, and drain on paper towels. Serve hot.

PICADOR'S CROQUETTES
CROQUETILLAS DE PICADOR

This is a crispy, easy-to-make croquette.

MAKES ABOUT 36

2 pounds potatoes, scrubbed clean
oil for frying
1 medium onion, finely diced
1 bell pepper, roasted (page 183) and chopped
salt and freshly ground black pepper to taste
pinch nutmeg
all-purpose flour for dredging
2 eggs, slightly beaten
1 cup fresh bread crumbs

1. Preheat the oven to 400°F. Bake the potatoes for 30 minutes in the hot oven. Pierce each potato with a fork to release any steam. Return to the oven, and bake for 30 minutes longer, or until easily pierced with a fork. Cut the potatoes in half, scoop out the flesh with a spoon, place in a bowl, and mash to a smooth puree. Discard the skins.

2. Heat ⅓ cup oil in a large skillet. Add the onion, and sauté until transparent. Add the roasted pepper, and sauté for a few seconds over high heat. Remove the onion and pepper from the skillet with a slotted spoon, drain on a paper towel, and place in a mixing bowl. Mash the onions and pepper together with a fork, and add to the mashed potatoes. Season with salt, pepper, and nutmeg, and blend well.

3. Scoop up small portions of the potato mixture with a teaspoon, and make bite-size balls. Roll the balls in the flour to coat. Dip the balls in the egg, then roll them in the bread crumbs to cover. (The croquettes may be prepared up to this point in advance and refrigerated until a few minutes before frying.)

4. Pour oil into a large skillet to ½ inch deep, and heat. Fry the croquettes in the hot oil until golden. Drain on paper towels, and serve hot.

BANDERILLAS (Pinchos)

Banderillas—or *pinchos*, as they are also called—are scrumptious tidbits of food, cooked or raw, threaded onto a toothpick or tiny skewer and served as an accompaniment with a mug of beer, a glass of manzanilla sherry, or the drink of your choice. They are named of course after the colorfully festooned darts traditionally used to tease the bull at the start of a *corrida de toro*, or bullfight, and, likewise, this version pleasantly teases the appetite.

Banderillas can be prepared at whim, using any favorite food or whatever is at hand. A few suggestions follow:

Black olives
Clams
Anchovies
Smoked herring
Marinated tuna (in *escabeche*, page 182, or in oil)
Smelts
Shrimp
Sausage
Hard-boiled eggs
Mussels

Pickles
Thin rolls of roasted sweet red pepper (page 183)
Chorizo sausage
Serrano ham
Cheese
Asparagus
Prawns
Rolls of ham stuffed with ensaladilla
Sardines in oil

Simply slide one or two bite-size portions of these foods onto toothpicks or tiny skewers, and serve garnished with chopped hard-boiled egg, chopped fresh parsley, or finely diced tomato. The following creations should inspire you further!

FRIED BANDERILLA ASSORTMENT
BANDERILLAS EN FRITURA

MAKES ABOUT 20

1 pound hake, bones and skin removed, cut into bite-size cubes
4 sweet peppers, roasted (page 183), cut into bite-size pieces
1 large onion, coarsely chopped
salt and freshly ground black pepper
oil for frying
all-purpose flour for dredging
2 eggs, slightly beaten

1. Thread the pieces of hake, roasted pepper, and onion on small (5- or 6-inch) wooden or metal skewers, alternating the pieces and finishing with the hake. Season each skewer with salt and pepper to taste.

2. Pour oil into a large skillet to ¼ inch deep and heat. Roll the tiny skewers in the flour, then dip in the egg to coat. Place the skewers in the hot oil and fry over moderate heat, turning to brown evenly on all sides. Remove from the skillet, and drain on paper towels. Serve hot.

NOTE: If desired, roll the skewers in fresh bread crumbs to coat after dipping in the egg.

CHICKEN BREAST PINCHOS WITH FOIE GRAS
PINCHOS DE PECHUGA DE AVE

MAKES ABOUT 36

2 boneless, skinless chicken breasts
1 medium onion, coarsely chopped
1 carrot, peeled and halved
1 bouquet garni
1 celery stalk, halved
oil for frying
all-purpose flour for dredging
2 eggs, slightly beaten

1. Place the chicken breasts, onion, carrot, bouquet garni, and celery in a saucepan with water to cover. Cover, and bring to a boil. Uncover, lower heat, and simmer for 30 minutes. Remove the chicken, transfer to a cutting board, and slice into ¾-inch-thick bite-size fillets. Skewer the fillets on toothpicks or tiny skewers, and spread with a small amount of pâté.

2. Pour oil into a large skillet to ¼ inch deep, and heat. Dredge the pinchos in the flour, and dip in the egg. Fry in the hot oil until golden, drain on paper towels, and serve.

"RASTRO" SANDWICHES
EMPAREDADOS DEL RASTRO

SERVES 8

oil for frying
2 slices sandwich bread, crusts removed, and cut into 4 triangles
    each
4 tomatoes
salt
1 6½-ounce can tuna, marinated (page 182)
8 round slices peeled cucumber

1. Pour a small amount of oil into a skillet. When hot, fry the bread until browned on both sides.

2. Slice the tomatoes in half. Season with salt to taste. Place a small amount of tuna on each tomato half. Top with a slice of cucumber, and salt again if desired. Place 1 bread triangle on top of the cucumber, skewer all layers together with a toothpick, and serve.

PINCHOS SARRAU

Thread cleaned whole mushrooms and bacon onto skewers, brush with oil, and place on a hot grill, barbecue, or under an oven broiler. Cook, turning occasionally, until the mushrooms are tender and the bacon is sizzling and browned. Remove from the grill or oven, and serve.

CHORIZO AND ONION PINCHOS
PINCHOS DE CHORIZO Y CEBOLLA

MAKES ABOUT 36

1 large onion, quartered lengthwise
1 bouquet garni
salt to taste
½ teaspoon sugar
1 teaspoon paprika
3 tablespoons olive oil
1 pound chorizo, thinly sliced

1. Separate the layers of the quartered onion, and place them in a skillet with water to barely cover. Add the bouquet garni, salt, sugar, paprika, and oil. Place over high heat, and cook until the water is evaporated. Remove the onion from heat, and set aside.

2. Heat the grill. Skewer chorizo slices and 2 pieces of onion at a time on toothpicks or tiny skewers. Place the pinchos on the hot grill or barbecue or under the oven broiler, and cook until browned evenly. Serve hot.

SPICY MINTY LAMB KEBOBS
PINCHITOS MORUNOS (Chonah Keftah)

SERVES 12

1 teaspoon sugar
1 fresh mint leaf
3 tablespoons white wine
1 red cherry pepper (or substitute), seeded, deveined, and diced
salt (optional)
1½–2 pounds lamb shoulder, cut into 1-inch cubes
oil for frying or grilling
1 teaspoon sweet or spicy paprika, or ½ teaspoon each
   (available in specialty shops)

1. Mash the sugar and mint leaf in a mortar, until a fine paste is formed. Add the wine, and stir to dissolve the sugar. Season with the pimenta moruna and salt, if desired. Place the lamb in a glass or stainless steel bowl. Spoon the sugar and mint mixture over the lamb, and toss to coat. Marinate for 2 to 3 hours in the refrigerator.

2. Heat the grill. Skewer the lamb onto small (4-inch) skewers, brush with oil, and place on the hot grill, barbecue, or under a broiler, turning occasionally to brown on all sides, 4 to 5 minutes each side. Cook to taste.

VARIATION: Prepare the mint mixture and reserve. Pour oil into a large skillet to ¼ inch deep, and heat. Fry the skewered lamb, turning occasionally until browned evenly on all sides, and cooked to taste. Set aside. Add the paprika to the remaining oil, and cook, stirring vigorously to prevent mixture from burning. Add the mint mixture and cook until the sauce begins to simmer. Remove from heat, and scrape into a bowl. Pass the fried skewered lamb with the sauce for dunking.

ROAST PORK PINCHOS
PINCHOS DE LOMO DE CERDO

MAKES 15 TO 20

1 pound pork shoulder or loin, cut into 2-inch cubes
2 sweet red peppers, roasted (page 183), cut into bite-size
    squares
⅓ cup olive oil
1 cup tomato sauce (page 173), heated

1. Heat the grill. Skewer the pork cubes alternating with pieces of roasted red pepper on toothpicks or tiny skewers. Dip the pinchos in the oil to coat, and roast them until browned, 10 to 15 minutes, on the grill, barbecue, or under the oven broiler.

2. Place the pinchos on a serving platter, and pass with the tomato sauce.

MUSSEL AND CURED HAM PINCHOS
PINCHOS DE MEJILLONES CON JAMON

MAKES ABOUT 24

2 pounds mussels, cleaned (page 181)
½ pound Serrano ham or prosciutto, thinly sliced and cut into
    3"- × -1" strips
salt and freshly ground black pepper
½ cup olive oil

1. Place the mussels in a saucepan with water to cover. Cover
and place over high heat. Cook until all shells are opened. Remove from heat. Remove each mussel from its shell. Wrap each
mussel in a strip of ham, and skewer on toothpicks or tiny
skewers. Season with salt and pepper to taste, and brush with
the oil.

2. Place the pinchos on a hot grill or barbecue, or under an oven
broiler, and cook for 1 minute, rotating once. Remove from heat
and serve.

PUFF PASTRY DOUGH
BAKED HERBED RABBIT IN PUFF PASTRY
SMOKED HERRING IN PUFF PASTRY
CODFISH IN PUFF PASTRY
SPICY STEWED BEEF IN PUFF PASTRY
SWEETBREADS AND ONION IN PUFF PASTRY
HAM AND CHICKEN CURLS
LITTLE CHEESE AND PASTRY SNAILS
WILD MUSHROOM PASTRIES
TOASTY BANANA KERCHIEFS
CHAMBERILERA ONION TART

2.

PUFF PASTRY, EMPANADILLAS, AND TAPAS ON TOAST

EMPANADILLA PASTRY DOUGH
TUNA EMPANADILLAS
SAVORY SAUSAGE EMPANADILLAS
SARDINE EMPANADILLAS
MALLORCAN COCARROIS
LITTLE GOLDEN CHEESE PIES
CATALONIAN SPICED SAUSAGE CAPS
ANCHOVY TOAST
CHORIZO TOAST
FLAMENCO SPREAD
HAM AND RED PEPPER SANDWICHES

Hundreds of tapas are made with pastry or served with bread. Flaky pastry or toast points form the perfect cradle for spiced, stewed meats, melted cheese, vegetables, or thick hearty meat spreads. But far more significant than the pastries or breads with which they are served are the savory fillings in the tapa recipes in this chapter: wild mushrooms, spicy chorizo sausage, anchovies, and sautéed onions with olives are just a few of the classic fillings.

In Spain and other Mediterranean countries pastry doughs are still prepared with lard instead of butter or even vegetable shortening. For the pastry recipes that follow, one of these three shortenings is suggested—however, any one can be substituted for any other, or combinations used if preferred.

For tapas on toast, always use the finest quality dense white bread available.

PUFF PASTRY DOUGH
PASTA DE HOJALDRE

MAKES ABOUT THIRTY 2½-INCH DOUBLE CRUST
PASTRY TARTLETS
OR 80 2-INCH SINGLE CRUST PASTRY SQUARES

3 cups all-purpose flour
¾ cup cold water
1 teaspoon salt
1 tablespoon white vine vinegar
1 tablespoon plus 2 sticks (½ pound) sweet butter, chilled (see Variation)
1 egg, slightly beaten

1. Place the flour in a mound on a table or countertop. Make a well in the center, and add the water, salt, vinegar, and 1 tablespoon butter, broken into pieces. Using your hands, mix well, blending in the flour a little at a time, and taking care not to overwork the dough. Knead gently for 1 minute, and form the dough into a ball. Cut an X in the top of the dough ball with the tip of a knife, and let rest in a warm place for 30 minutes.

2. On a lightly floured surface, roll the dough out into a 16"- × - 12" rectangle, about ⅛ inch thick. Slice the remaining butter into ¼-inch-thick pats, and place on top of one half the dough. Fold the other half of the dough over the butter, and roll it out into a ⅛-inch-thick rectangle. Fold the dough in thirds from front to back. Then, fold in thirds from right to left. Place the dough on a tray or cutting board, put a plate or platter on top, and chill for 15 minutes. Roll out again into a rectangle, and repeat the folding process. Weight the dough again and chill for another 15 minutes. The dough is now ready to use as required in the Puff Pastry recipes.

VARIATION: Substitute margarine for the butter, or 1 stick (¼ pound) plus 7 tablespoons margarine plus 1 tablespoon of lard, mixing in the lard in step 1.

Costraditas (tartlets):

1. Roll the dough out onto a lightly floured surface into a large circle, about 20 inches in diameter and ⅛ inch thick. Cut out 60 pastry circles with a 2½-inch cookie cutter, and line tiny 2½-inch tart tins with half the pastry circles, reserving the other half for the top crusts. Prick the shells with a fork, and fill.

2. Preheat the oven to 400°F. Brush the edges of the pastry tarts with some egg, fill as desired, then top with the reserved pastry circles. Pinch or press the edges together to seal. Brush the tops of the pastries with the egg.

3. Place the pastries on a cookie sheet and bake for 5 minutes. Lower heat to 375° and bake for 15 to 20 minutes longer, or until golden. Remove from the oven and let cool for 10 minutes. Remove the pastries from the tins and serve warm.

Pastry Squares:

1. Roll out the dough on a lightly floured surface into an 18"- × - 18" rectangle about ⅛ inch thick. With a pastry wheel, cut out about 80 squares approximately 2" × 2". Top with the desired filling, roll up and fill, or fill and pinch the corners together, as described on the following pages. Brush with the egg.

2. Preheat the oven to 400°F. Place the pastries on a cookie sheet sprinkled with water. Bake as for Costraditas above.

BAKED HERBED RABBIT IN PUFF PASTRY
COSTRADITAS DE CONEJO

MAKES ABOUT 30

2 pounds rabbit meat, cut into serving pieces
1 cup coarsely chopped onion
1 whole head garlic, each clove peeled
1 bouquet garni
1 teaspoon paprika
⅓ cup white wine
⅓ cup olive oil
3 tablespoons red wine vinegar
salt and freshly ground black pepper to taste
1 cup water
1 teaspoon all-purpose flour mixed with 2 tablespoons cold
    water (optional)
Puff Pastry Dough (page 35)

1. Preheat the oven to 375°F.

2. Place the rabbit in a large casserole or deep baking dish. Add the next 8 ingredients. Cover and bake for about 30 minutes, or until the liquid is evaporated. Add the water and bake for 30 to 45 minutes longer, or until the rabbit is tender. Remove the meat from the sauce with a slotted spoon. Debone the rabbit pieces and chop or shred the meat into small pieces to fill the pastries. Set aside. Remove the herbs and garlic from the sauce and discard.

3. If the remaining sauce is too thin, pour it into a saucepan, and thicken it by adding the flour-water mixture. Bring to a boil over medium heat, stirring constantly. Remove from heat and correct the seasonings. If desired, strain the sauce to remove large pieces of onion. Reserve.

4. Prepare Costraditas as described on page 36. Fill each with 1 heaping teaspoon meat and 1 teaspoon sauce. Bake as directed.

NOTE: To stretch the meat filling for more pastry shells, use less rabbit meat for each shell and add a thin slice of roasted sweet red pepper [page 183 per pastry].

SMOKED HERRING IN PUFF PASTRY
COSTRADITAS DE ARENQUES A LA INGLESA

MAKES ABOUT 30

1 recipe Puff Pastry Dough (page 35)
1 pound smoked herring fillets, cut into 1"- × -3" strips
1 recipe Tomato Sauce (page 173)
1 tablespoon cognac

1. Roll and cut pastry dough as for Costraditas (page 36).

2. To make English Sauce, reduce one recipe Tomato Sauce until thickened and stir in 1 tablespoon cognac.

3. Roll the herring fillets into small tight rolls that will fit the tiny pastry shells. Place 1 roll in the center of each pastry shell. Cover with 1 teaspoon English Sauce.

4. Follow the instructions to complete the Costraditas and bake as directed.

CODFISH IN PUFF PASTRY
COSTRADITAS DE BACALAO

MAKES ABOUT 30

2 pounds dried salt cod (page 180), prepared 1 day in advance
¼ cup olive or vegetable oil
1 clove garlic
2 to 3 strands saffron
1 tablespoon finely chopped fresh parsley
1-pound can tomatoes, peeled, drained, and chopped
pinch sugar
salt and freshly ground pepper to taste
1 recipe Puff Pastry Dough (page 35)

1. Preheat the oven to 400°F and grease a baking dish. Place the cod in the dish and bake for 20 minutes, or until the meat is white all through at the thickest point. Remove the cod from the oven and flake, removing and discarding the skin and bones. Place the cod in a colander and rinse under lukewarm water. Drain well and reserve.

2. Heat the oil in a skillet or clay casserole (*cazuela de barro*). Add the garlic, and sauté until golden. Mash together the saffron and parsley in a mortar and pestle and add to the sautéed garlic with the tomatoes, sugar, and seasonings. Simmer for 15 minutes, stirring occasionally.

3. Add the cod to the sauce and simmer for 5 minutes. Cover and set aside.

4. Roll out the pastry dough as for Costraditas (page 36) and prepare tiny pie tins. Fill each pastry shell with 1 tablespoon cod and 2 teaspoons sauce.

5. Follow the instructions to complete the Costraditas and bake as directed.

SPICY STEWED BEEF IN PUFF PASTRY
COSTRADITAS DE CARNE A LA DIABLA

A thick, spicy tomato-based sauce makes for a distinctive tapa.

MAKES ABOUT 30

1 recipe Puff Pastry Dough (page 35)
2 pounds beef shank, all visible fat removed
2 quarts water
1 large carrot
1 large leek
1 stalk celery, cut into thirds

Brown Sauce:

1 tablespoon butter
1 tablespoon all-purpose flour, lightly toasted in a skillet
2 cups beef broth from beef shank

Hot Sauce:

⅓ cup white wine
1 heaping tablespoon finely chopped shallot
⅓ cup tomato paste
1 teaspoon red wine vinegar
1 teaspoon finely chopped fresh parsley
1 teaspoon cayenne pepper, or to taste
1 teaspoon Dijon mustard

1. Roll out the pastry dough as directed for Costraditas (page 36), and line tiny pie tins. Set aside.

2. Place the meat in a large saucepan with the water (the bone from the beef shank may also be added for a richer broth). Add the carrot, leek, and celery. Bring to a boil, lower heat, and simmer gently for 4 to 5 hours, adding more water as needed. Reserve 2 cups of the broth. Cover and set aside to prepare the brown sauce.

3. To make the brown sauce, melt the butter in a small saucepan. Slowly stir in the flour, blending well. Stir in the 2 cups beef broth, and bring to a boil. Lower heat and simmer, stirring constantly, for 10 minutes. Set aside.

4. To prepare the hot sauce, place the wine and shallot in a saucepan. Cook over medium heat until reduced by half. Add the tomato paste and brown sauce, blending well. Simmer for 5 minutes, stirring occasionally. Add the vinegar, parsley, cayenne, and mustard. Remove from heat.

5. Place the stewed meat on a cutting board and chop or shred into very small pieces. Fill each pastry shell with 1 tablespoon meat. Pour 2 teaspoons hot sauce over the meat in each shell.

6. Follow the instructions to complete the Costraditas and bake as directed.

SWEETBREADS AND ONION IN PUFF PASTRY
COSTRADITAS DE MOLLEJAS

MAKES ABOUT 30

1 recipe Puff Pastry Dough (page 35)
3 calf sweetbreads
1 cup finely chopped onions
2 medium carrots, cut into very thin 1-inch strips
1 cup coarsely chopped tomato
1 bouquet garni
⅓ cup olive oil
⅓ cup white wine
2 cups water
1 teaspoon cornstarch

1. Preheat the oven to 350°F. Roll out the pastry dough and line tiny pie tins as for Costraditas (page 36).

2. Soak the sweetbreads in cold water to cover, changing the water frequently, until all blood is drained and the water is clear. Drain well.

3. Place the sweetbreads in a saucepan with cold water to cover. Bring to a boil over high heat. Remove from heat immediately, drain and refresh under cold running water. Place the sweetbreads on a cutting board, remove and discard nerves and any visible fat.

4. Place the onion, carrots, tomato, and bouquet garni in the bottom of a large casserole or baking dish and layer the sweetbreads on top. Pour the oil over the meat and vegetables, stir once to mix, and cover. Bake for 8 to 10 minutes, or until the vegetables begin to brown. Remove the casserole from the oven and skim off any fat that has drained to the bottom of the casserole. Add the wine, return the casserole to the oven, and bake until all liquid has evaporated, about 10 to 15 minutes. Add 1 cup water and bake for 30 minutes longer. Remove from the oven.

5. Remove the sweetbreads from the casserole and chop into small pieces. Discard bouquet garni. Leave the oven on.

6. Pour the remaining sauce and vegetables into a small saucepan (or leave in the casserole if it can be heated on the stovetop). Dissolve the cornstarch in 1 cup water and add to the sauce, stirring constantly over medium heat. Bring to a boil and continue stirring until thickened. Reserve.

7. Place 1 tablespoon chopped sweetbreads and 2 teaspoons sauce in each pastry.

8. Follow the instructions to complete the Costraditas and bake as directed.

NOTE: In step 6, the sauce can also be strained to remove the vegetables, if desired. To thicken the strained sauce, dissolve 1 to 2 teaspoons all-purpose flour in 1 cup water and add to the sauce, stirring, over medium heat. Bring to a boil and stir in 2 slightly beaten egg yolks, blending well.

HAM AND CHICKEN CURLS
COSTRADITAS DE JAMÓN Y POLLO

MAKES ABOUT 30

1 boneless, skinless chicken breast
1 small onion, coarsely chopped
½ carrot, peeled
1 bouquet garni
½ stalk celery
2 cups water
2 teaspoons butter
1 heaping teaspoon all-purpose flour
10 strips bacon, cooked until browned but not crisp, and cut into
    thirds, or thirty 1"-×-3" strips of Serrano ham
1 recipe Puff Pastry Dough (page 35)

1. Place the chicken breast in a saucepan with the onion, carrot, bouquet garni, celery, and water. Cover, and bring to a boil. Uncover, lower heat, and simmer for 30 minutes. Remove the chicken, and transfer to a cutting board. Simmer the broth until reduced to ⅓ to ½ cup. Stir in the butter and flour, blending well. Cook for 1 minute longer, or until thickened. Remove from heat.

2. Cut the chicken breast into small cubes or strips. Wrap a few pieces of the chicken in each slice of bacon or ham. Set aside.

3. Roll out and cut the dough as for Costraditas (page 36).

4. Place one portion of the chicken pieces wrapped in bacon or ham in the center of each tart shell. Top each portion with 1 teaspoon of the thickened chicken broth.

5. Follow the instructions to complete the Costraditas, and bake as directed.

LITTLE CHEESE AND PASTRY SNAILS
CARACOLILLOS DE HOJALDRE Y QUESO

MAKES ABOUT 42

½ recipe Puff Pastry Dough (page 35)
1 pound Manchego, Bola, or Gruyère cheese, cut into ½"-×-2"
    strips
1 egg, slightly beaten

1. Preheat the oven to 400°F. Roll out the dough on a lightly floured surface into a 9"-×-18" rectangle about ⅛-inch thick. With a pastry wheel, cut out about forty-two 1½"-×-2½" rectangles.

2. Place 1 piece of cheese at one end of each rectangle and roll up the pastries.

3. Place the pastries on a cookie sheet sprinkled with water. Brush the fold with the egg and press to seal with your fingertips. Brush the rest of the surface with the egg. Bake the pastries for 5 minutes. Lower heat to 375°F and bake for 10 to 13 minutes longer, until golden.

WILD MUSHROOM PASTRIES
MONTERAS O MONTERILLAS

MAKES ABOUT 60

2 cloves garlic, minced
1 heaping tablespoon finely chopped fresh parsley
6 tablespoons olive or vegetable oil
60 wild mushrooms (porcini and shiitaki mushrooms work well)
    about 2-inch-wide caps, washed and destemmed
1 recipe Puff Pastry Dough (page 35)
1 egg, slightly beaten

1. Mix the garlic and parsley and set aside.

2. Heat 3 tablespoons olive oil in a skillet. Add the mushrooms and stir until they release their juice, 5 to 8 minutes. Drain the juice from the skillet, and reserve the mushrooms. Add 3 more tablespoons oil to the skillet, and heat. Return the mushrooms to the skillet, and continue to stir. Add the garlic and parsley mixture. Stir-fry for 1 minute longer, and remove from heat.

3. Preheat the oven to 400°F. On a lightly floured surface, roll the pastry dough into a 20-inch circle, about ⅛" thick. With a pastry wheel or 2½-inch round cookie cutter cut out 60 2½-inch circles. Place the pastry circles on a cookie sheet sprinkled with water.

4. Place 1 mushroom in the center of each circle. Brush the edges of the pastry with the egg. Bake the mushroom pastries for 5 minutes. Lower heat to 375° and bake for 8 minutes longer, or until golden. Remove from the oven, cool slightly, and serve.

VARIATION: You can add 2 tablespoons pureed tomatoes to the mushrooms with the garlic.

TOASTY BANANA KERCHIEFS
PAÑUELITOS DE HOJALDRE Y PLATANO

MAKES ABOUT 36

½ recipe Puff Pastry Dough (page 35)
2 ripe firm bananas, sliced into 10 to 12 rounds each
1 egg, slightly beaten

1. Preheat the oven to 400°F. On a lightly floured surface, roll out the pastry dough into a 9″-by-18″ rectangle about ⅛ inch thick. With a pastry wheel or knife, cut out about thirty-six 2-inch squares.

2. Place 1 banana slice in the center of each square. Brush the edges of the squares with the egg, and bring up the sides of the square to the center, pressing the edges together to seal and form a "kerchief." Place the pastries on a baking sheet sprinkled with water, and brush with more egg. Bake for 5 minutes. Lower heat to 375° and bake for 13 to 15 minutes longer, or until golden. Serve hot.

NOTE: The pastries may also be fried in oil until golden.

CHAMBERILERA ONION TART
TARTA CHAMBERILERA

Light, elegant, and simple, this tapa is named for the picturesque Madrid neighborhood of Chamberí, known for its beautiful architecture and classical Castilian customs.

SERVES 8 TO 10

1 recipe Puff Pastry Dough (page 35)
½ cup olive or vegetable oil
1 clove garlic, diced
1 pound onions, very thinly sliced
7 to 10 anchovy fillets

7 to 10 large pitted black olives
1 egg, slightly beaten

1. Preheat the oven to 400°F.

2. Divide the dough into 2 parts. On a lightly floured surface, roll out one-half of the dough into a circle 10 to 11 inches in diameter. Line a shallow 9- to 10-inch tart pan with the pastry, or place the pastry on a pizza tin or cookie sheet drizzled with cold water. Set aside.

3. Heat the oil in a large skillet. Add the garlic and the onion, cover, and sauté over moderate heat until the onion begins to brown. Remove from heat, and discard the garlic. Remove the onions from the skillet with a slotted spoon, draining well, and spread them on the pastry circle to within ¼ inch from the outer edges.

4. Wrap 1 anchovy fillet around each olive, and arrange in a circle around the center of the tart. Roll out the remaining pastry and place it over the onion-olive-anchovy filling. Seal the edges with the tines of a fork, or fold the edges together under the tart, if using a tart pan. Poke holes in the top of the tart with a fork to allow steam to escape.

5. Brush the pastry with the egg, and bake for 5 minutes. Lower heat to 375°, and bake for 20 to 25 minutes longer, or until golden.

VARIATION: ½ pound peeled, seeded, and chopped tomatoes may be added to the onions a few minutes after beginning to sauté, together with 1 heaping teaspoon flour and a pinch sugar. Blend well, and continue to sauté until the onions begin to brown.

EMPANADILLA PASTRY DOUGH
Empanadillas

Empanadillas are dainty pastry turnovers filled with chopped fish, beef, sausage, ham, poultry, game, or green vegetables. The fillings are usually mixed with sautéed tomatoes, bechamel, or meat sauces. These fried pastries are flaky, light, and savory, but baking is always an option for the calorie conscious. They can be served hot or cold, but are best hot. This recipe for Empanadilla Pastry Dough and method for making empanadillas can be used with any of the fillings described on the following pages.

MAKES ABOUT 30

3 cups all-purpose flour
2 level teaspoons dry yeast
6 tablespoons chilled vegetable shortening or lard
1 teaspoon salt
½ cup lukewarm milk
1 egg
pinch freshly ground white pepper
pinch grated nutmeg
oil for frying
1 egg, slightly beaten (optional)

1. Place the flour and yeast in a large bowl and combine. Make a well in the center, and add the next 6 ingredients. Mix together well until a smooth dough is formed. Form 2 balls with the dough, brush the surfaces lightly with oil, and cut an X in the top of each ball with the tip of a knife. Cover with a dish towel or bowl, and let rest in a warm place for 30 minutes.

2. On a lightly floured surface, roll out each dough ball to ⅛ inch thick. With a fluted pastry wheel or cookie cutter, cut out pastry circles 2½ to 3 inches in diameter. Place 1 level teaspoon of filling in the center of each circle. Brush the edges of the circles with a small amount of water, and fold in half over the filling to form half-moon shapes. Seal the edges by pressing together with the tines of a fork. Brush the tops of the pastries with the slightly beaten egg, if desired.

3. Pour the oil for frying into a large skillet to ½ inch deep, and heat. Fry the empanadillas in the hot oil until golden. Drain on paper towels, and serve.

NOTE: Empanadillas may be baked instead of fried. To bake, preheat the over to 375°F and place the pastries on a lightly greased cookie sheet and bake for 15 to 18 minutes. When rolling the dough for empanadillas which are to be baked, it is preferable to roll it just slightly thicker than for pastries to be fried.

TUNA EMPANADILLAS
EMPANADILLAS DE ATUN

SERVES 4 TO 6

1 recipe Empanadilla Pastry Dough (page 48)
3 tablespoons olive or vegetable oil
1 clove garlic
1 1-pound can peeled tomatoes, drained well and diced
salt to taste
pinch sugar
1 heaping teaspoon all-purpose flour
1 teaspoon paprika
1 6½-ounce can albacore or chunk light tuna, drained and
   flaked

1. Prepare the empanadilla pastry dough.

2. Heat the olive oil in a large skillet. Add the garlic and sauté until golden. Remove the garlic with a slotted spoon and discard. Add the tomatoes, season with salt and sugar, cover, and simmer for 10 minutes over low heat, stirring occasionally. Stir in the flour and paprika, blending well. Add the tuna, and stir to combine all ingredients. Simmer for 5 minutes longer and remove from heat.

3. Complete the Empanadillas as directed.

VARIATION: Add 1 cup very thinly sliced roasted sweet red pepper (page 183) to the mixture when adding the tuna.

SAVORY SAUSAGE EMPANADILLAS
EMPANADILLAS DE EMBUTIDOS

SERVES 4 TO 6

1 recipe Empanadilla Pastry Dough (page 48)
½ pound chorizo, sobrasada, or other smoked sausage, cut into
   ⅛- to ¼-inch slices

1. Roll out and cut the dough as directed.

2. Place 1 or 2 slices of sausage just off the center of each pastry circle.

3. Form the empanadillas and fry or bake as directed.

SARDINE EMPANADILLAS
EMPANADILLAS DE SARDINAS

SERVES 4 TO 6

1 recipe Empanadilla Pastry Dough (page 48)
½ pound fresh sardines, cleaned (page 181)
3 tablespoons olive or vegetable oil
1 clove garlic, minced
1 pound beefy, ripe tomatoes, seeded and chopped
salt to taste
pinch sugar

1. Prepare the dough as directed.

2. Place the fillets in a baking dish, and set aside.

3. Preheat the oven to 425°F. Heat the olive oil in a skillet. Add the garlic, and sauté for just a few seconds. Add the tomatoes. Season with salt and sugar. Cover and simmer over low heat until the juice from the tomatoes is completely evaporated, about 10 minutes. Remove from heat. Spread the sauce evenly over the sardine fillets, and bake for 10 minutes, or until the sardines are flaky and white at the thickest part.

4. Turn the sauce-covered fillets onto a cutting board. Chop the fillets into fine pieces, forming a smooth paste. Place the mixture in a bowl. Correct the seasonings, and set aside.

5. Fill each circle with 1 even tablespoon of the sardine filling and continue to assemble, and fry or bake the empanadillas as directed.

LITTLE GOLDEN CHEESE PIES
PASTELES DE QUESO

These golden, light little pies are very distinctive and very easy to make. The cheesy, almost sweet filling melts in the mouth. They are best right out of the oven, but keep well.

MAKES ABOUT EIGHTEEN 2- TO 2½-INCH TARTLETS

⅔ cup all-purpose flour
½ teaspoon dry yeast
2 teaspoons salt
3½ tablespoons chilled butter, broken into small bits
2 eggs, separated
1 tablespoon milk, plus 1 cup plus 3 tablespoons warm milk
2 cups grated Parmesan, Cheddar, Bola, Gruyère, or Manchego cheese
6 tablespoons cornstarch
1 cup heavy cream
1 teaspoon sugar

1. Sift the flour, yeast, and 1 teaspoon salt together in a mixing bowl. Cut in the butter until the mixture resembles small peas. Add the egg whites and 1 tablespoon milk, and mix together with a fork, using a few swift strokes, until all the dry ingredients are moistened. Turn the dough onto a lightly floured surface, and knead gently for 3 to 5 minutes, or until smooth and elastic. Cover with a cloth or bowl, and let rest for 15 minutes.

2. Place 1⅔ cups cheese, the egg yolks, cornstarch, cream, 1 cup warm milk, 1 teaspoon salt, and sugar in a saucepan. Whisk together and place over low heat. Cook, stirring constantly, until the mixture is thickened. Add the remaining 3 tablespoons milk, stir well to blend, and remove from heat. Set aside.

3. Preheat the oven to 350°F. Roll out the dough on a lightly floured surface to ⅛ inch thick. Line eighteen 2- to 2½-inch pie tins with the pastry. Prick the pastries with a fork several times. Fill each pastry with the cheese mixture, and sprinkle with the remaining ⅓ cup grated cheese.

4. Place the pastries on a cookie sheet, and bake for 25 to 30 minutes, or until the crust is lightly browned and the cheese filling is golden and puffy. Remove the pastries from the oven, and let cool for 5 minutes. Remove the pastries from the tins, and serve hot or at room temperature.

NOTE: About a half recipe of Puff Pastry Dough (page 35) may be used instead of the pastry dough described in this recipe.

CATALONIAN SPICED SAUSAGE CAPS
BARRETINAS CATALANAS

Barretinas are the typical pointed red felt caps worn by the men of Cataloña, and Butifarra is the sweet garlic sausage of the region. Polish kielbasa is a good substitute.

MAKES ABOUT 30

3 tablespoons olive oil
½ pound onions, sliced into thin rounds
2 tablespoons paprika, or 1 tablespoon sweet and 1 tablespoon spicy (available in specialty shops)
1 pound Butifarra pork sausages, cut into 1-inch pieces
⅓ cup red wine (Priorato is nice)
1 recipe Empanadilla Pastry Dough (page 48)
1 egg, slightly beaten
¼ cup vegetable oil
¼ cup lard

1. Heat the 3 tablespoons olive oil in a skillet. Add the onions, and sauté until tender. Add the paprika, and blend well. Add the sausage. Drizzle the wine over all the ingredients, and toss to combine. Cook until the wine is evaporated and the sausage is cooked through, 15 to 20 minutes.

2. On a lightly floured surface, roll out the pastry dough to ⅛ inch thick. With a pastry wheel or knife, cut out rectangles 3″ × 2″. Place 1 sausage piece with 1 teaspoon stewed onion mixture at one narrow end of each rectangle, and roll up to form a pipe shape. Seal the edges by brushing lightly with the egg and pressing together with fingertips. Set aside.

3. Heat the vegetable oil and the lard in a skillet. Place the "caps" in the skillet, and fry until golden. Remove, and drain on paper towels. Serve hot.

ANCHOVY TOAST
DARTAIS DE ANCHOAS

SERVES 6 TO 8

4 slices of good-quality white bread, crusts removed
½ cup homemade mayonnaise (page 172)
4 2-ounce cans anchovy fillets, drained
Fresh parsley sprigs for garnish

1. Preheat the oven to 375°F.

2. Cut the bread slices into ½"- × -3" strips. Place the strips on a cookie sheet and bake until lightly toasted.

3. Spread each toasted bread strip with a thin layer of mayonnaise. Top with 1 anchovy.

4. Arrange on a serving platter and garnish with parsley.

CHORIZO TOAST
MONTAITOS DE CHORIZO

MAKES 24

24 ¼-inch slices chorizo sausage
6 slices of good-quality white bread, crusts removed
oil for frying
½ cup warmed tomato sauce (page 173)

1. Preheat the oven to 400°F.

2. Place the chorizo in a roasting pan, and roast for about 10 minutes, or until sizzling.

3. Cut the bread slices into 4 squares each. Pour oil into a skillet to ¼ inch deep, and heat. Fry the bread squares until golden, turning once. Remove, and drain on paper towels.

4. Place a dab of tomato sauce in the center of each bread square and spread, almost to edges. Place 1 slice of chorizo in the center of each square. Spear the squares with toothpicks and serve.

FLAMENCO SPREAD
PICADILLO FLAMENCO

This nicely seasoned spread based on ground pork and ham goes a long way. It can be prepared in advance and keeps well.

MAKES 40 TO 60

vegetable oil for frying
½ cup finely diced cooked ham
½ pound lean ground pork
2 pounds onions, thinly sliced
1 bouquet garni
2 pounds tomatoes, seeded and diced
salt and freshly ground black pepper to taste
½ teaspoon sugar
½ cup fresh bread crumbs
25 toasted almonds (page 18)
1 teaspoon finely chopped fresh parsley
2 to 3 strands of saffron
⅓ cup water
10 to 15 slices of good-quality white sandwich bread, crusts removed, sliced into 4 squares each

1. Heat ⅓ cup vegetable oil in a large skillet. Add the ham and pork and toss together over medium heat until lightly browned. Drain off 2 tablespoons of the oil into a medium-size skillet and set aside. Stir in the onions and bouquet garni, and sauté until the onion is transparent but not browned. Add the tomatoes, and season with salt, pepper, and sugar. Simmer over low heat for 15 minutes, stirring occasionally. Set aside.

2. Place the bread crumbs in the small skillet with the reserved oil used to fry the ham and pork, and cook over medium heat, stirring constantly, until lightly toasted. Place the toasted bread crumbs, almonds, parsley, and saffron in a mortar and mash together with a pestle. Add the mixture to the meat and vegetables. Stir in the water, correct the seasonings to taste, and let simmer for 15 minutes longer, stirring occasionally.

3. Pour the oil for frying into a large skillet to barely ¼ inch deep, and heat. Fry the bread squares in the hot oil until golden on both sides, and drain on paper towels. Spread the minced pork and ham mixture on the bread squares and serve.

HAM AND RED PEPPER SANDWICHES
EMPAREDADOS FLAMENCOS DE JAMÓN Y PIMIENTO FRITO

MAKES 12

1 loaf French bread, sliced into 24 ¼-inch slices
3 tablespoons soft butter
12 thin slices cured ham. Serrano is best, if available, or
   prosciutto
12 slices sweet red pepper, roasted (page 183)
freshly ground black pepper, grated nutmeg, and ground cloves
   to taste
oil for frying
1 cup milk
1 cup all-purpose flour
3 eggs, slightly beaten

1. Place the bread slices on a cutting board or countertop and spread 1 side of each slice with the butter. Top the buttered side with 1 slice of ham and 1 slice of roasted pepper. Season to taste with the pepper, nutmeg, and cloves. Top each with the remaining slices of buttered bread, buttered side down.

2. In a large skillet pour the oil to ⅛ inch deep, and heat. Pour the milk into a shallow bowl, and place each sandwich in the milk, turning to coat. Dust the sandwiches with the flour, then dip them in the egg to coat. Place the sandwiches in the hot oil, and fry until golden on both sides.

3. Drain the sandwiches on a paper towel, and serve hot.

NOTE: You may also use chopped ham and chopped peppers in place of slices.

BATTER-FRIED ARTICHOKES

RONDA-STYLE GREEN BEANS

CASSEROLE OF BROAD BEANS AND ARTICHOKES

GRILLED WILD MUSHROOMS

MUSHROOMS IN GARLIC SAUCE

ANCHOVIES WITH CAPERS

ROASTED RED PEPPERS STUFFED WITH SAUSAGE

3.

GOLDEN OVEN-FRIED NEW POTATOES

SPICY POTATOES

VEGETABLE TAPAS AND APPETIZING SALADS

BAKED POTATO MORSELS WITH SHRIMP

TUNA-STUFFED TOMATOES

SALMON-STUFFED TOMATOES

SHREDDED CHICKEN BREAST AND OLIVES ON ESCAROLE
WITH ONION VINAIGRETTE

POTATO-ALMOND SALAD WITH ANDALUSIAN VINAIGRETTE

SALAD OCCIDENTAL WITH WORCESTERSHIRE DRESSING

ENSALADILLA MADRID

POTATO SALAD WITH FRESH MINT AND CITRUS MAYONNAISE

For the vegetable lover, Spain offers some surprising variations on the basic bean, potato, and tomato. Dressed up with olive oil and capers, or stuffed with sausage, tuna, and shrimp, vegetable tapas are wonderful combinations of taste, texture, and color. Even salads with mixtures that celebrate their Iberian origins— chicken breast with olives or potatoes and almonds—can be served as tapas: simply pass around small servings on tiny plates.

Vegetable tapas such as oven-fried potatoes or grilled mushrooms are fine complements for skewered or stewed meats or fish tapas, while other vegetable tapas—succulent roasted red peppers stuffed with spicy sausage meat or juicy whole tomatoes filled with tuna or salmon—stand on their own and can be the centerpiece of a tapa party. Even home-marinated olives are a memorable tapa, not to be overlooked for the sake of more complicated dishes. And of course vegetable and salad tapas offer an alternative for lighter snacking as well as variety on a tableful of meat, fish, and egg dishes.

BATTER-FRIED ARTICHOKES
ALCACHOFAS REBOZADAS

This is a Mediterranean classic.

MAKES 12

12 tender artichokes, trunks removed
1 quart cold water
½ lemon
1 bay leaf
pinch dried thyme
¼ teaspoon white pepper
2 tablespoons olive oil
salt
oil for frying
all-purpose flour for dredging
4 eggs, slightly beaten

1. Remove the thick green outer leaves from each artichoke, leaving the soft fleshy leaves and heart only. Trim the base to remove the thick section of the leaves. Cut off the leaves about halfway down to remove the thick tips and thorns. Carefully spread the center leaves apart, and scoop out the choke with the tip of a spoon. Rub each artichoke with the cut side of the lemon to prevent discoloration. Place the artichokes in a large saucepan with the water. Add the lemon half (used or fresh). Add the bay leaf, thyme, white pepper, olive oil, and salt to taste. Cover, and place over high heat. Bring to a boil. Lower heat, and simmer for 15 to 20 minutes, or until the artichokes are tender and an outer leaf is easily removed. (The artichokes may be prepared in advance up to this point, placed in a glass or earthenware dish with the cooking liquid, covered, and refrigerated for up to 2 days.)

2. Pour the oil for frying into a skillet to ⅛ inch deep, and heat. Drain the artichokes well. Slice each artichoke in half or in quarters. Dredge the pieces in the flour, then dip in the egg to coat. Fry the artichokes in the hot oil until golden. Drain on a paper towel, and serve hot.

NOTE: The artichokes may be rolled in fresh bread crumbs just after being coated with the egg, then fried.

RONDA-STYLE GREEN BEANS
HABAS A LA RONDENA

SERVES 4 TO 6
(Recipe can be halved)

An Andalusian specialty.

2 pounds broad green beans, shelled
salt
⅓ cup olive or vegetable oil
2 cloves garlic, finely chopped
4 ounces cooked ham, diced
½ pound tomatoes, seeded and diced
freshly ground black pepper
2 eggs, hard-boiled, halved

1. Rinse the beans in a colander under cold running water, and drain. Place them in a pot with water to cover and 1 tablespoon salt. Cover, and bring to a boil. Reduce heat, and simmer for 30 to 40 minutes, or until tender. Drain, reserving ⅓ cup of the liquid, and return the beans to the pot.

2. Heat the oil in a saucepan. Add the garlic and ham, and sauté until the garlic is golden. Add the tomatoes, and simmer for 5 minutes. Season with salt and pepper to taste, and pour the mixture over the beans. Add the reserved cooking liquid, and place over medium heat. Cook for 5 minutes. Remove from heat, and transfer the beans to a serving dish. Garnish with the hard-boiled egg halves, and serve.

CASSEROLE OF BROAD BEANS AND ARTICHOKES
CAZUELITA DE HABAS VERDES A LA GRANADINA

SERVES 4 TO 6

A mélange of cumin-and-mint-enhanced vegetables coats these broad beans to their best advantage.

1½ pounds broad green beans, hulled
1 tablespoon salt
1 10-ounce package frozen artichoke hearts
¼ cup olive or vegetable oil
2 cloves garlic, chopped
1 medium onion, finely chopped
½ pound tomatoes, peeled, seeded, and chopped
1 bouquet garni
2 to 3 strands of saffron
½ teaspoon ground cumin
½ teaspoon dried mint leaves, or 2 to 3 fresh leaves
¼ cup fresh bread crumbs browned in 1 tablespoon oil

1. Preheat the oven to 375°F.

2. Rinse the beans well under cold running water, and drain. Place them in a pot with water to cover. Add the salt. Cover, and bring to a boil. Reduce heat, and simmer for 20 to 30 minutes, or until tender. Drain, reserving ⅓ cup of the liquid, and place the beans with the reserved liquid in a large casserole. Set aside.

3. While the beans are simmering, cook the artichoke hearts in ⅓ cup boiling salted water for 3 to 6 minutes. Drain well, reserving 3 tablespoons of the liquid.

4. Heat the oil in a large skillet. Add the garlic, then the onions, tomatoes, and bouquet garni. Cook over low heat for 10 minutes, stirring occasionally.

5. Make a picada of the saffron, cumin, mint leaves, and fried bread crumbs in a mortar. Blend in 3 tablespoons of the reserved liquid from the artichokes to form a paste. Stir the picada into the sautéing vegetables.

6. Pour the vegetables over the cooked beans, and toss. Cover the casserole and bake for 5 minutes. Toss again with the artichoke hearts, and serve.

GRILLED WILD MUSHROOMS
SETAS A LA PLANCHA

SERVES 8

Substitute one of the more usual varieties if you like. (The result will still be delicious!)

2 pounds large wild mushrooms (porcini and shiitaki work well)
salt
olive oil

1. Heat the grill. Cut the stems from the mushrooms, and clean the caps under cold running water. Drain well. Season with salt to taste, and brush with olive oil.

2. Place the mushrooms on a hot but not sizzling grill or barbecue, or under the oven broiler. Cook until browned, turning frequently. Remove from heat, and serve.

VARIATIONS: Grilled Mushrooms are delicious served with Aioli. For a quick and easy Aioli, prepare mayonnaise (page 172), adding 2 cloves minced garlic to the egg yolks, vinegar, salt, and pepper before adding the oil.

They also can be dipped in a sauce prepared with oil, garlic, and parsley: For 2 pounds mushrooms, heat ⅓ cup olive oil in a skillet. Add 1 clove minced garlic, and sauté until golden. Add 1 tablespoon finely chopped fresh parsley and 1 tablespoon fresh bread crumbs, stirring well to blend. Serve with the mushrooms.

MUSHROOMS IN GARLIC SAUCE
CHAMPIÑONES AL AJILLO

SERVES 4 TO 6

⅓ cup olive or vegetable oil
3 cloves garlic, 2 finely chopped
1 pound mushrooms, washed well, destemmed
1 teaspoon finely chopped fresh parsley
salt and freshly ground black pepper

Heat the oil in a large skillet until hot but not sizzling. Add 1 whole clove garlic, then the mushrooms, and sauté for 1 minute, stirring constantly, or until the juice given off by the mushrooms evaporates. Add the chopped garlic and parsley. Combine all the ingredients, season with salt and pepper to taste, and serve.

ANCHOVIES WITH CAPERS
FILETES DE ANCHOAS CON ALCAPARRAS

SERVES 10 TO 12

3 2-ounce cans anchovy fillets, drained
about 60 small capers
¼ cup fine-quality olive oil
1 sweet red pepper, roasted (page 183), cut into very thin strips
⅓ cup finely chopped fresh parsley

1. Place 2 to 3 capers in the center of each anchovy fillet and roll the fillet tightly.

2. Place the fillets on a serving dish and drizzle with the olive oil. Garnish with the pepper strips and sprinkle with parsley.

ROASTED RED PEPPERS STUFFED WITH SAUSAGE
CANUTILLOS RIOJANOS

The sweet red peppers complement the salty pork, an unusual variation on the typical sausage-and-pepper dish. Pretty to look at, a first-class finger food, and easy to make.

MAKES 12 TO 16

1 tablespoon olive or vegetable oil
1 clove garlic, finely chopped
1 tablespoon finely chopped onion
1 teaspoon finely chopped fresh parsley
6 ounces finely ground pork sausage meat
½ egg, slightly beaten
1 tablespoon white wine
salt and freshly ground black pepper
pinch grated nutmeg
3 to 4 large red bell peppers, roasted (page 183)
⅓ cup vinaigrette A or C (pages 177 and 178) or homemade
   mayonnaise (page 172)

1. Preheat the oven to 425°F, and lightly grease a baking dish.

2. Heat the oil in a small skillet. Add the garlic and onion, and sauté until tender. Stir in the parsley, and mix well. Remove from heat, and let cool.

3. Combine the sausage meat, egg, and the garlic-onion mixture in a bowl and mix well. Add the wine, salt and pepper to taste, and nutmeg, and combine well. Set aside.

4. Slice each roasted pepper lengthwise into 4 equal strips. Place 1 teaspoon sausage stuffing at one edge of each pepper slice, and roll the slices up into "flute" form. Place the stuffed peppers in the baking dish, and bake for 10 to 12 minutes, or until the stuffing is cooked through and not pink inside. Remove the peppers from the oven, and let cool slightly.

5. Drizzle with the vinaigrette or spread the tops with a thin layer of mayonnaise, if desired, and serve.

GOLDEN OVEN-FRIED NEW POTATOES
LAS PATATAS DORADAS

SERVES 4

½ pound very small potatoes (new potatoes, if available), peeled and halved
salt
3 tablespoons olive oil
3½ tablespoons butter, melted

1. Place the potatoes in a saucepan with cold water to cover. Add 1 teaspoon salt, place over high heat, and bring to a boil. Simmer for 5 to 8 minutes.

2. Preheat the oven to 375°F. Drain the potatoes, and place them in a baking dish. Pour the oil and butter over the potatoes, and toss. Season with salt to taste. Bake for 10 to 15 minutes, or until golden and easily pierced with a fork.

SPICY POTATOES
PATATAS PICANTES

SERVES 6 TO 8

oil for frying
1 clove garlic
1 heaping teaspoon finely chopped onion
2 to 3 parsley stems, chopped
1 heaping teaspoon all-purpose flour
1 teaspoon spicy paprika (available in specialty shops)
5 ounces plum tomatoes, seeded and chopped
1 bay leaf
1 teaspoon sugar
1 teaspoon salt
1 cup water
1 pound small potatoes (about the size of an egg), peeled

1. Heat 2 tablespoons oil in a saucepan. Sauté the garlic, onion, and parsley stems in the hot oil until the onion is transparent, but not browned. Stir in the flour and paprika, blending well. Add the tomatoes, bay leaf, sugar, and salt. Cook over low heat for 10 minutes, stirring occasionally. Add the water, blend well, and cook for 2 to 5 minutes longer. Remove from heat, and strain the sauce through a colander into a bowl. Set aside.

2. Slice the potatoes in half lengthwise. Slice each half into 2 or 3 slices or into cubes. Rinse in cold water, drain well, and pat dry. Pour the oil into a large skillet to ¼ inch deep, and heat. Place the potatoes in the oil, one layer at a time, and fry until tender but not browned. Remove with a slotted spoon, and drain on paper towels.

3. Just before serving, reheat the remaining oil in the skillet until very hot (add more as needed to fill the skillet to ¼ inch with oil). Fry the potatoes in the oil until crispy, but not entirely browned. Remove with a slotted spoon, drain well, and serve with the spicy sauce.

BAKED POTATO MORSELS WITH SHRIMP
LAS EXQUISITAS PATATAS CON GAMBAS

SERVES 8 TO 12

2 pounds potatoes, peeled
oil for frying
salt and freshly ground white pepper
flour for dredging
2 eggs, slightly beaten
12 large shrimp, shelled and deveined
1 bouquet garni
1 egg, hard-boiled, finely chopped
¼ cup finely chopped fresh parsley

1. Preheat the oven to 350°F. Slice the potatoes into ¼-inch-thick rounds.

2. Pour oil into a large skillet to ¼ inch deep, and heat. Season the potatoes with salt and white pepper to taste, dredge in the flour, and dip in the egg. Place the rounds in the hot oil, and fry until soft, but not browned. Remove from the skillet, and transfer to a casserole or baking dish.

3. Sprinkle the potatoes with the shrimp. Add water to barely cover the bouquet garni. Bake for 25 minutes. Remove from the oven, and let cool for 10 minutes. Sprinkle with chopped egg and parsley, and serve.

TUNA-STUFFED TOMATOES
TOMATES RELLENOS DE ATUN

SERVES 6

6 large firm-ripe tomatoes
salt
sugar
freshly ground black pepper
1 6½-ounce can white albacore tuna, drained and flaked
1 cup béchamel sauce (page 175) (see Note)
1 tablespoon grated Gruyère, Cheddar, or Bola cheese
2 tablespoons butter, melted, tossed with 1 tablespoon finely
   chopped fresh parsley

1. Preheat the oven to 350°F.

2. Slice a thin layer off the top of each tomato. With a spoon, gently scoop out the tomato pulp, and discard. Season the tomatoes with the salt, sugar, and pepper to taste. Place, open side down, on a rack to drain well.

3. Combine the tuna with ¾ cup white sauce, and fill the tomatoes with this mixture. Top the tomatoes with the remaining white sauce, and sprinkle with the cheese, and parsley-butter. Place on a baking sheet and bake until the cheese is melted, about 5 minutes. Remove and serve.

NOTE: 1 cup homemade mayonnaise (page 172) may be substituted for the rich béchamel.

SALMON-STUFFED TOMATOES
TOMATES RELLENOS

MAKES 6 TO 10 SERVINGS

6 to 10 large firm-ripe tomatoes
salt
1 15½-ounce can salmon, drained and flaked
6 leaves lettuce, washed, patted dry, and shredded
¾ cup homemade mayonnaise (page 172)
2 eggs, hard-boiled, finely chopped

1. Slice the tops off the tomatoes. Gently scoop out the pulp and seeds. Season with salt and turn the tomatoes open end down on a rack or in a colander to drain.

2. Place the salmon in a small bowl. Add the lettuce and mayonnaise, and mix well.

3. Fill the tomatoes with the salmon mixture. Place on a serving dish, and chill until ready to serve. Just before serving, sprinkle the tops with the chopped egg.

SALADS

SHREDDED CHICKEN BREAST AND OLIVES ON ESCAROLE WITH ONION VINAIGRETTE
ENSALADA CORDOBESA

SERVES 4 TO 6

1 large head escarole, leaves washed and patted dry
1 boneless, skinless chicken breast, poached and shredded
3 tablespoons anchovy-stuffed olives
2 tablespoons pimento-stuffed olives
crust from 1 thick piece Italian or French bread, rubbed with 1
    clove garlic
1 cup watercress, washed and patted dry

Onion Vinaigrette:
1 small onion (or scallion), finely chopped
1 teaspoon salt
2 tablespoons white wine vinegar
3 tablespoons olive oil
1 tablespoon water

1. Tear the escarole into bite-size pieces and place in layers in a large salad bowl or platter. Cover with the chicken pieces. Combine the olives, and sprinkle over the chicken. Break the bread crust into small cubes, and sprinkle over the salad. Garnish the edges of the bowl or platter with the watercress. Refrigerate the salad until ready to serve.

2. To make the vinaigrette, place the onion and salt in a mortar, and mash together to form a paste. Add the vinegar, oil, and water. Moments before serving the salad, whisk the vinaigrette until the ingredients are emulsified. Pour over the salad, and serve.

73

POTATO-ALMOND SALAD WITH ANDALUSIAN VINAIGRETTE
ENSALADA "MANHATTAN" CON VINAGRETA ANDALUZA

SERVES 6

½ pound potatoes, scrubbed clean
1 tablespoon salt
⅓ cup heavy cream
12 toasted almonds, crushed, mixed with 2 tablespoons orange juice
⅓ cup fresh spinach leaves, rinsed and patted dry
1 heart of celery, sliced into 1-inch julienne
3 pearl onions, thinly sliced

Vinaigrette:

3 tablespoons olive oil
2 tablespoons white wine vinegar
1 tablespoon water
1 tablespoon tomato paste

1. Place the potatoes in a saucepan with water to cover and the salt. Cover, and bring to a boil. Cook for 20 to 30 minutes, or until the potatoes can be easily pierced with a fork. Remove from heat, and let cool in the cooking liquid. Peel the potatoes, and slice lengthwise into ½-inch-wide strips. Place the potato strips in a large salad bowl. Add the cream and crushed almond–orange juice mixture. Toss well to combine.

2. Tear the spinach leaves into bite-size pieces. Line the edges of the salad bowl with the leaves. Arrange the celery strips on top of the spinach, then sprinkle with the sliced onion. Chill the salad until moments before serving.

3. Combine the vinaigrette ingredients in a small bowl or measuring cup. Moments before serving the salad, whisk the vinaigrette until the ingredients are emulsified. Pour over the salad greens, and toss. Top with the potato-and-almond mixture, and serve.

SALAD OCCIDENTAL WITH WORCESTERSHIRE DRESSING
ENSALADA OCCIDENTAL

SERVES 6

1 clove garlic
½ pound asparagus
1 head escarole, leaves washed and patted dry
1 heart of small cabbage, shredded
1 small onion, thinly sliced
6 tablespoons olive oil
3 tablespoons lemon juice
1 teaspoon salt
½ teaspoon freshly ground black pepper
1 teaspoon Worcestershire sauce
3½ ounces grated Parmesan cheese
1 cup croutons
12 anchovy fillets, finely diced

1. Rub the inside of a large salad bowl with the clove of garlic, and set aside.

2. Snap off and discard the woody ends of the asparagus and place the spears in a pot of boiling salted water to cover. Cook for 3 to 6 minutes, or until just crisp-tender. Drain and immediately place in a bowl of ice water, and set aside until cool. Drain well, and cut into 1-inch pieces. Place in the salad bowl.

3. Tear the escarole into bite-size pieces, and place in the salad bowl with the asparagus. Add the cabbage and onion. Toss to combine, and refrigerate until ready to serve.

4. Just before serving, combine the oil, lemon juice, salt, pepper, and Worcestershire sauce in a small bowl or measuring cup, mixing well.

5. Sprinkle the salad with the cheese, croutons, and anchovies. Pour the dressing over the salad, toss well, and serve.

ENSALADILLA MADRID

SERVES 4 TO 6

2 quarts water
salt to taste
½ pound fresh peas, shucked
2 medium carrots, diced
½ pound potatoes, scrubbed clean
1 recipe mayonnaise (page 172) prepared with 1 cup oil and 1
   egg
2 eggs, hard-boiled, sliced (optional)
chopped fresh parsley (optional)

1. In a large saucepan bring the water with salt to a boil, add the peas, and cook for 15 to 20 minutes, until tender but not over-cooked. Drain and refresh under cold running water. Place the peas on a clean dish towel to drain completely, leaving space to drain the carrots.

2. In another saucepan cook the carrots in boiling salted water to cover over low heat for 10 to 15 minutes or until crisp-tender. Drain, and refresh under cold running water. Place the carrots alongside the peas to drain completely on the dish towel.

3. Place the potatoes in a saucepan with salted water to cover and bring to a boil. Cook for 20 to 30 minutes, or until they can be pierced easily with a fork. Drain well, and fill the saucepan with cold water to cover the potatoes. Let the potatoes cool in the water until they can be handled easily. Peel and dice the potatoes.

4. Combine all the cooked vegetables in a large bowl. Add the mayonnaise and mix well. Garnish with the hard-boiled egg slices and parsley, if desired.

POTATO SALAD WITH FRESH MINT AND CITRUS MAYONNAISE
ENSALADILLA VALENCIANA

SERVES 8

2 pounds potatoes, scrubbed clean
salt
1 medium onion, thinly sliced
2 hearts of lettuce, shredded
freshly ground black pepper
5 to 6 fresh mint leaves, chopped
juice of ½ orange
juice of ½ lemon
½ cup homemade mayonnaise (page 172) or ½ cup vinaigrette
   (page 74)
2 eggs, hard-boiled, sliced

1. Place the potatoes in a saucepan with water to cover. Add 1 teaspoon salt. Cover, bring to a boil. Reduce heat and simmer for 20 to 30 minutes, or until the potatoes are tender but still firm. Remove from heat, and let cool in the cooking water. When cool enough to handle, drain well, and peel.

2. Cut the potatoes into thin strips or small dice, and place them in a large bowl. Add the onion and hearts of lettuce. Toss well to combine. Add salt and pepper to taste, the mint, orange and lemon juices, and toss. Add the mayonnaise or vinaigrette, and mix well. Chill until ready to serve. Moments before serving garnish with slices of hard-boiled egg.

VARIATION: 1 cup chopped cooked shellfish—shrimp, prawns, lobster, or a combination—may be added to any of these salads.

GRILLED TUNA STEAKS WITH ANCHOVY BUTTER
GRILLED MARINATED BLUE-FIN TUNA STEAKS
BAKED TUNA WITH GARLIC DRESSING
CASSEROLE OF MARINATED BLUE-FIN TUNA AND PISTO
MARINATED BLUE-FIN TUNA IN TOMATO SAUCE
CASSEROLE OF TUNA STEAKS AND TENDER STRAW POTATOES
CHILLED TUNA BALLS
LITTLE PAVIAN SOLDIERS
MULETEER-STYLE FLAKED COD WITH GARLIC
POACHED COD WITH AIOLI
SAUTÉED COD WITH ONIONS AND HERBS
FLAKED COD WITH NEW POTATOES

FISH TAPAS

COD IN CREAMY GARLIC SAUCE
COD WITH CURED HAM AND HOT RED PEPPERS
BAKED MONKFISH WITH PEAS AND GARLIC-SAFFRON SAUCE
MONKFISH IN BASQUE SAUCE
MONKFISH IN ALMOND SAUCE
QUICK-FRIED MONKFISH
HAKE MORSELS SAN SEBASTIAN
HAKE MORSELS IN GREEN SAUCE
FRESH SARDINES STUFFED WITH SPINACH AND MUSSELS
FRESH SARDINES IN TOMATO-SHERRY SAUCE
SARDINE ROLLS OVIEDO WITH GREEN PEPPER SAUCE
BARBECUED SARDINES STEAMED IN LETTUCE
SQUID IN BLACK SAUCE
GOLDEN BATTER-FRIED SQUID
OCTOPUS FOR A SAINT'S DAY FEAST
CRISPY BREADED ANCHOVIES
FRIED EEL
BARBECUED EEL ON SKEWERS

Some of the best-known bars in coastal areas specialize in seafood, including some varieties which can be found in no other
part of the world. Even inland, fish tapas are a staple in the bars
and taverns. Codfish, hake, and sardines are celebrated from
San Sebastian to Alicante with an impressive array of fresh
sauces, unusual stuffings, and diverse cooking methods that
show off the qualities of each variety of fish to best advantage.
The richness and color of fish tapas make them ideal as the
centerpiece of a very festive tapas meal.

It is perhaps the northern coast that sustains the richest reper-
toire of fish tapa recipes. In the Cantabrian provinces of Asturias,
Santander, and Galicia (home to a thriving fishing industry and
to a rich culinary marriage between Northern European cooking
with its sophisticated sauces and Mediterranean cuisine's intimate
knowledge of olive oil, garlic, and rice), fish is treated to an enor-
mous variation of colorful and delicious preparations, and the
result flaunted on the counters of tapas bars. Galicia in particular
is known for its marinated and sauced sardines, Asturias for succulent fish and vegetable stews, Santander for its sauces and its
glorious codfish preparations. On the Mediterranean coast, Catalan cooking celebrates *parilladas*, or mixed fish grills seasoned
with lemon, olive oil, and spices.

Not all of the fish required in the following
recipes are available everywhere in the United
States, but acceptable substitutes can be used
and, as always, the fresher the better.

GRILLED TUNA STEAKS WITH ANCHOVY BUTTER
ATUN EN FILETES DE RIBADEO

Juicy, tangy, and savory.

MAKES 12 PIECES

6 anchovies
2 tablespoons butter, at room temperature
1 pound fresh tuna, cut into 12 thin fillets
2 tablespoons olive oil
salt

1. Mash the anchovies in a mortar. Add the butter, and mix well to make a smooth spread. Set aside.

2. Brush the tuna fillets with the oil, and season with salt to taste. Cook the steaks on a kitchen grill, in the oven broiler, or on an outdoor barbecue, just a few minutes on each side. (Take care not to overcook because the fish will become very dry.) Serve the steaks sizzling hot accompanied with the anchovy spread.

GRILLED MARINATED BLUE-FIN TUNA STEAKS
BONITO EN PARRILLA A LA GALLEGA

This dish is lovely with new potatoes.

SERVES 6 TO 8

2 pounds blue-fin tuna steaks
3 cloves garlic
1 tablespoon chopped fresh parsley
1 teaspoon paprika
2 tablespoons white wine vinegar
3 tablespoons olive oil
⅓ cup white wine

1. Place the fish in a glass or stainless steel bowl.

2. Mash the garlic and parsley in a mortar. Stir in the paprika. Transfer to small mixing bowl. Add the vinegar and oil, mixing well. Stir in the white wine, and pour the ingredients over the fish, tossing to coat each steak. Refrigerate, and let marinate, covered, for 1 hour.

3. Prepare the grill. (The fish can be marinated up to 1 day before grilling.) Remove the steaks from the marinade, and place on the hot grill. Cook on both sides until the meat is white and flaky.

BAKED TUNA WITH GARLIC DRESSING
HIJADAS DE ATUN ASADAS

SERVES 8

1 pound tuna steak, cut into serving pieces
salt
½ cup fresh bread crumbs
2 cloves garlic, chopped
½ cup finely chopped fresh parsley
3 tablespoons olive oil

1. Place the fish in a baking dish, and salt to taste.

2. Preheat the oven to 400°F. In a bowl combine the bread crumbs, garlic, and parsley. Sprinkle the mixture over the fish, and drizzle with the oil. Place the fish in the oven, and bake for 5 minutes. Lower heat to 375° and bake for 5 to 10 minutes more, or until the skin is golden brown and the flesh is flaky white. Serve immediately.

CASSEROLE OF MARINATED BLUE-FIN TUNA AND PISTO
BONITO EN ESCABECHE CON PISTO

The ingredients for Pisto, a classic summer vegetable casserole prepared throughout Spain, vary from region to region. Pisto almost always includes tomato, red peppers, and zucchini squash, but the use of potatoes is indigenous to the (tlk) region. On the Iberian peninsula, Pisto is almost as celebrated as its famous international cousin, gazpacho!

SERVES 8 TO 10

Pisto Sauce:

⅓ cup olive oil
2 cloves garlic
2 medium onions, thinly sliced
½ pound potatoes, peeled and sliced into 2-inch strawlike strips
2 zucchini or eggplant or combination (about 1½ pounds), cut into thin 1-inch strips
salt and freshly ground black pepper
1 pound tomatoes, peeled, seeded, and finely chopped
pinch sugar
⅓ cup fish (page 181) or vegetable broth
2 pounds blue-fin tuna steaks, cut into small serving pieces
chopped fresh parsley

1. To make the sauce, pour the oil in a large skillet or saucepan and heat. Add the garlic and sauté until golden. Add the onions, potatoes, and squash and/or eggplant. Season with salt and pepper to taste, and sauté until the onion is wilted. Add the tomatoes, sugar, and broth, cover, and simmer for 10 to 12 minutes. Check the seasonings, adding more salt and pepper, if desired. Cover, and simmer for 5 minutes longer. Remove from heat.

2. Preheat the oven to 400°F. Place the tuna pieces in a large shallow casserole or baking dish. Pour the pisto sauce over the tuna. Place the casserole in the oven and bake for 5 minutes. Lower heat to 375° and bake for 10 to 15 minutes longer, or until the fish appears white when pierced with a fork. Sprinkle with the parsley, and serve.

VARIATIONS: Add thin strips of roasted pepper (page 183) when adding the onions, potatoes, and squash or eggplant to sauté.
Stir in 1 teaspoon paprika just before adding the tomatoes.
Sauté 2 ounces finely diced ham with the garlic before adding the vegetables.

MARINATED BLUE-FIN TUNA IN TOMATO SAUCE
BONITO EN ESCABECHE CON TOMATE

SERVES 8 TO 10

½ cup olive oil
3 cloves garlic
3 sprigs parsley, plus ¼ cup finely chopped parsley
3 tablespoons white wine vinegar
3 tablespoons white wine
1⅓ cups water
1 bay leaf
2 to 3 black peppercorns
2 pounds blue-fin tuna steaks, cut into small serving pieces
2 cups tomato sauce (page 173)
salt (optional)

1. To prepare the marinade, heat 3 tablespoons oil in a skillet. Add 2 cloves garlic, and sauté until tender. Add the 3 sprigs parsley and the vinegar, mixing well. Stir in the wine, 1 cup water, bay leaf, and peppercorns, and simmer gently for 5 minutes. Set aside.

2. Preheat the oven to 400°F. Place the tuna pieces in a large casserole or baking dish. Mash the remaining garlic clove, combine with the remaining olive oil, and pour over the fish. Cover the tuna with the tomato sauce, and sprinkle with the chopped parsley. Next, pour the marinade and ⅓ cup water over the fish. Place the tuna in the oven, and bake for 5 minutes. Lower heat to 375°, and bake for 10 to 15 minutes longer. Season with salt, if desired, and serve.

CASSEROLE OF TUNA STEAKS AND TENDER STRAW POTATOES
ATUN CON PATATAS EN CAZUELA

SERVES 8

1 pound tuna steaks, cut into serving pieces
⅓ cup vegetable or olive oil
1½ pounds potatoes, peeled and sliced into thin straws
salt and freshly ground black pepper
1 clove garlic, finely chopped
3 tablespoons finely chopped onion
½ teaspoon paprika
1 teaspoon all-purpose flour
3 cups boiling water

1. Brush the tuna pieces lightly with oil and set aside.

2. Season the potatoes with salt and pepper to taste. Cover the bottom of a deep casserole or baking dish with one layer of potatoes. Top with half of the tuna. Repeat the layers, ending with a layer of potatoes. Set aside.

3. Preheat the oven to 350°F. Heat the remaining oil in a large saucepan. Add the garlic and onion, and sauté until the onion is wilted but not browned. Stir in the paprika and flour, blending well. Stir in the water, and bring the mixture to a boil. Remove from heat. Add more salt and pepper to taste. Pour the mixture over the layered tuna and potatoes. Place the casserole in the oven, and bake for 30 to 40 minutes, or until the potatoes are tender.

CHILLED TUNA BALLS
BOLITAS DE ATUN

SERVES 4 TO 6

½ cup dry bread crumbs soaked in 2 tablespoons milk
1 tablespoon finely chopped fresh parsley, plus extra for garnish
3 eggs, hard-boiled, yolks and whites separated
1 6½-ounce can albacore or chunk light tuna, drained and
    flaked
2 tablespoons grated Parmesan cheese
5 tablespoons butter, at room temperature
salt and freshly ground black pepper
5 to 6 lettuce leaves, washed and patted dry
⅓ cup homemade mayonnaise (page 172)

1. Place the bread crumbs, parsley, and egg yolks in a bowl and blend well with a fork. Add the tuna, blend again. Add the cheese, and then the butter, 1 tablespoon at a time, blending well after each addition. Season with salt and pepper to taste.

2. Line a serving platter with the lettuce leaves. Scoop up heaping teaspoonsful of the tuna paste and roll into bite-size balls. Arrange the balls decoratively on top of the lettuce leaves.

3. Spread a thin layer of mayonnaise on the top of each tuna ball. Chop the egg white into very fine pieces and sprinkle over the tuna balls. Garnish with finely chopped parsley. Chill until ready to serve.

LITTLE PAVIAN SOLDIERS
SOLDADITOS DE PAVIA

"Little Pavian Soldiers" are strips of marinated and spiced codfish, batter-dipped, and fried until golden and crisp.

MAKES ABOUT 16 SERVINGS

1 pound dried salt cod (page 180) (thin pieces are best)
1 clove garlic
salt
2 sprigs parsley
3 strands of saffron
2 tablespoons cold water
1 teaspoon lemon juice
1¼ cups all-purpose flour
2 teaspoons baking powder
pinch freshly ground white pepper
vegetable oil for frying
¾ cup milk

1. Cut the dried cod fillets into 2"- × -¾"–1" strips thick, and place the strips in a glass or stainless steel bowl. Make a *picada* of the garlic, salt, parsley, and saffron in a mortar. Dilute the paste with the cold water. Stir in the lemon juice. Pour the mixture over the cod, mixing well to coat all the strips of fish. Cover and refrigerate for about 1 hour.

2. Place the flour, baking powder, pinch salt and white pepper in a bowl, combine, and form a well in the center. Add 3 table-spoons oil and milk, and mix with a few quick strokes until all the dry ingredients are moistened.

3. Pour the oil for frying into a large skillet to ½ inch deep, and heat until very hot. Dip the marinated cod strips in the batter to coat, and drop one by one in the hot oil. Fry just over 1 minute, or until golden on both sides. Drain on paper towels, and serve hot.

VARIATION: For added color and a spicier taste, serve the cod strips garnished with thin strips of roasted sweet red or green pepper (page 183) brushed with a thin coat of olive oil.

MULETEER-STYLE FLAKED COD WITH GARLIC
BACALAO AL AJO ARRIERO

SERVES 8 TO 10

2 pounds dried salt cod (page 180) (use thick pieces from body
    of fish)
½ cup olive or vegetable oil
2 cloves garlic, minced
1 large onion, thinly sliced
2 cups tomato sauce (page 173)
2 to 4 sweet red peppers, roasted (page 183), sliced into thin
    strips
salt

1. Flake the cod pieces and remove the skin and bones. Reserve.

2. Heat the oil in a large casserole or Dutch oven. Add the garlic,
then the onion. Sauté gently until the onion is transparent. Add
the tomato sauce, then the flaked cod, and mix well. Add the
pepper slices. Simmer for 10 to 15 minutes. Season with salt to
taste. Remove from heat, and let cool for 30 minutes before
serving.

POACHED COD WITH AIOLI
BACALAO AL AJOLIO O ALI-OLI

SERVES 8

1 pound dried salt cod (page 180)

Aioli:
2 cloves garlic, minced
1 egg yolk
½ to ¾ tablespoon white wine vinegar
salt and white pepper
1 cup olive oil
2 tablespoons cod broth

1. Cut the cod fillet into 8 square serving pieces. Place the fish in a pot with cold water to cover. Place the pot over moderate heat, and bring to a boil. Remove from heat, and let the cod cool in the cooking water. Reserve 2 tablespoons of the cooking broth for use in the aioli sauce.

2. To prepare the aioli, in a small bowl whisk together the garlic, egg yolk, vinegar, and salt and white pepper to taste. Add the oil in a slow, steady drizzle, whisking constantly until the mixture is emulsified. Pour the sauce into a small saucepan, and stir in 2 tablespoons of the reserved cooking broth from the cod. Heat through. Correct the seasonings. Remove from heat and reserve.

3. Remove the cod pieces from the pot with a slotted spoon, draining well, and place on a cutting board. Remove the skin and bones and slice the pieces into bite-size fillets. Place the cod on a serving dish. Pour half the aioli sauce over the fish, and toss lightly to coat. Pour the remaining aioli in a sauceboat or small bowl and pass with the cod.

NOTE: Boiled or baked new potatoes or small "red" potatoes are a fine accompaniment to this dish. To prepare, peel ½ pound potatoes, and place in a saucepan with water to cover. Add ½ tablespoon salt. Cover and bring to a boil. Cook for 30 minutes, drain, and serve with the cod.

SAUTÉED COD WITH ONIONS AND HERBS
BACALAO CON CEBOLLA

SERVES 8 TO 10

2 pounds dried salt cod (page 180) (thin pieces near tail are best)
⅓ cup olive or vegetable oil
2 medium onions, finely chopped or thinly sliced
1 clove garlic
1 heaping teaspoon finely chopped fresh parsley
1 bay leaf
2 teaspoons all-purpose flour
3 tablespoons white wine
salt and freshly ground black pepper

1. Cut the cod into 16 to 20 small serving pieces. Place the fish in a large pot with cold water to barely cover. Place over medium heat, and bring to a boil. Remove immediately from heat, and set aside to cool in cooking liquid. Once cooled completely, drain the cod, reserving 1 cup of the cooking liquid. Set aside.

2. Heat the oil in a large skillet or saucepan. Add the onion, garlic, parsley, and bay leaf, cover, and sauté over low heat until the onion is transparent but not browned. Stir in 1 teaspoon flour, and mix well. Add the cod to the onion mixture and stir in the wine, scraping up pieces of the sautéed onion and garlic mixture from the bottom and sides of the skillet as you stir. Cover, and simmer until the wine is evaporated.

3. Stir in the remaining flour. Blend well, and stir in half the reserved cooking liquid from the cod. Mix well, and add more liquid, if necessary, to obtain a light sauce. Season with salt and pepper to taste.

FLAKED COD WITH NEW POTATOES
BACALAO CON PATATAS NUEVAS

This is among the most delicious of all tapas, for my palate, as well as being one of the best to serve with fruity manzanilla wine, because of its superb taste and seasonings.

SERVES 8 TO 10

1 pound dried salt cod (page 180) (thick pieces from body of
  fish are best)
½ cup olive or vegetable oil
1 large onion, finely chopped
1 teaspoon all-purpose flour
2 pounds tiny new potatoes, peeled
salt and freshly ground black pepper
pinch ground cinnamon
1 clove garlic, mashed
1 bouquet garni
1 clove garlic, 1 tablespoon chopped fresh parsley, and 3 to 4
  strands of saffron, mashed together in a mortar
1 to 2 tablespoons cold water

1. Flake the cod and discard the skin and bones. Set aside.

2. Heat ⅓ cup oil in a small skillet. Add the onion and sauté, covered, over medium heat until transparent. Stir in the flour, blending well. Remove from heat. Pour mixture into the bowl of a food processor or blender, and puree. Reserve.

3. Season the potatoes with salt and pepper to taste and the cinnamon.

4. Heat the remaining oil in a large saucepan. Add the single clove of garlic, and the bouquet garni, and sauté until the garlic is golden. Add the cod, potatoes, and onion puree. Mix well, and add water to barely cover the potatoes.

5. Add the cold water to the mashed garlic, parsley, and saffron (picada), mixing well. Stir the *picada* into the saucepan with the cod and potatoes, and bring to a boil over high heat. Reduce to medium heat and simmer for 10 to 20 minutes, or until the potatoes are easily pierced with a fork. Remove from heat, let cool slightly, and serve.

COD IN CREAMY GARLIC SAUCE
CAZUELA DE BACALAO AL PIL-PIL

SERVES 8 TO 10

2 pounds dried salt cod (page 180)
2 cups olive or vegetable oil (see Notes)
4 large cloves garlic, finely chopped
⅓ cup milk (see Notes)
salt

1. Drain the cod well and cut into 16 to 20 small serving pieces. Place the fish in a large saucepan with cold water to cover. Place over moderate heat, and bring *almost* to the boiling point (do not let the water boil). Remove from heat immediately, and let the fish soak in the water for 30 minutes.

2. Pour the oil into a saucepan, and heat. Add the garlic. As the garlic begins to sauté, place the cod pieces, skin side down, in the saucepan, covering the bottom evenly. Slowly rotate the saucepan over the heat, so that the cod pieces slide around the bottom of the pan, scraping up pieces of the garlic as they move. Once the fish releases its gelatinous juices (after about 2 minutes) add the milk, while rotating the saucepan. Continue to rotate slowly until the mixture becomes creamy. After 10 to 12 minutes, flip the cod pieces so that skin sides are up. Season with salt to taste, and serve.

NOTES: At times, up to ½ cup milk may be necessary to obtain a creamy, but not too thick, sauce for the fish.
The sauce for the fish is best when the oil used is not very refined.

COD WITH CURED HAM AND HOT RED PEPPERS
CAZUELA DE BACALAO A LA VIZCAINA

Of all the recipes in our files, this one for cod from the Basque province of Vizcaya is one of the best and most classic. The salty crispy cod is spectacularly set off by a spicy hot pepper sauce. Almost better the second day. Faint of palate, beware!

SERVES 8 TO 10

2 pounds dried salt cod fillets (page 180) (thin fillets from the tail section of the fish are best)
12 dried hot red peppers (pasillas are good), seeded, stems removed
all-purpose flour for dredging
1 cup olive or vegetable oil
3 to 4 slices of white sandwich bread, cubed
2 ounces finely chopped cured Serrano ham or prosciutto
2 cloves garlic
1 bay leaf
1 pound onions, thinly sliced
1 heaping teaspoon paprika
salt
pinch sugar

1. Soak the cod with the dried hot peppers in fresh cold water for 24 hours, changing the water at least 3 times. Drain, reserving the peppers. Scrape off any scales remaining on the skin of the fish. Cut the fillets into small serving pieces (about twenty 1½-inch square pieces). Place the fillets in a large saucepan with cold water to cover, and place over high heat. Just as the water is about to boil, remove the saucepan from heat, and set aside. Let the fish cool for 10 to 15 minutes in the cooking liquid, then remove the fish with a slotted spoon and transfer to a cutting board. Reserve 1½ cups of the cooking liquid.

2. Remove any bones from the cod pieces. Dredge the fish in the flour, shaking off any excess.

3. Heat ⅓ cup oil in a large skillet. Fry the cod in the hot oil, a few minutes on each side, removing the pieces from the heat just before they begin to brown. Drain on paper towels. Arrange the fillets in a baking dish, skin side down.

4. Add the remaining oil to the skillet and heat. Place the bread cubes in the hot oil, and fry until golden on all sides. Add the ham, garlic, bay leaf, onions, and dried hot peppers. Cover, and sauté over low heat until the onion is transparent. Stir in the paprika, mixing well to combine all ingredients. Add 1 cup of the codfish cooking liquid, and bring the mixture to a boil. Cook for 10 minutes. Remove from heat.

5. Place the mixture in a food processor or blender, and puree until a fine paste is formed. Stir in more of the remaining broth, 1 tablespoon at a time, until the paste becomes a smooth sauce. Season with salt to taste and a pinch sugar, and puree a few seconds longer.

6. Preheat the oven to 400°F. Pour the sauce over the cod fillets, and bake for 15 to 20 minutes. Taking care not to force the oil to the top, as this will make the cod release more of its gelatin into the sauce, rotate the baking dish occasionally so that the fish will soak up the sauce and oil.

BAKED MONKFISH WITH PEAS AND GARLIC-SAFFRON SAUCE
FILETES DE RAPE CON GUISANTES

SERVES 8 TO 10

2 pounds thin monkfish fillets
salt
all-purpose flour
⅓ cup olive or vegetable oil for frying
2 eggs, slightly beaten
1 clove garlic
2 heaping tablespoons finely chopped onion
1 cup water
1 clove garlic and 2 to 3 strands of saffron mashed together
2 heaping tablespoons small cooked peas

1. Cut the monkfish into 16 to 20 serving pieces (not too small, however, because monkfish shrinks considerably when cooked). Season with salt to taste. Dredge the fillets in 1 cup flour, and set aside.

2. Pour the oil into a large skillet to ¼ inch deep, and heat. Dip the fillets in the egg to coat, and place them in the hot oil to fry until lightly browned. Add more oil as needed. Remove the fillets, and transfer to a baking dish.

3. Preheat the oven to 400°F. Add the garlic, chopped onion, and 1 teaspoon flour to the oil remaining in the skillet, and blend well over medium heat. Do not let the mixture brown. Stir in the water and the picada of garlic and saffron. Correct the seasonings, and pour over the fish (see Note). Sprinkle the peas on top, and bake the fish for 10 minutes.

NOTE: The sauce should be somewhat thick before pouring over the fish because the fish will give off its own liquid to thin it. If the sauce seems too thin after adding the garlic-saffron mixture, simmer it for a few minutes longer in the skillet to reduce before adding to the fish.

MONKFISH IN BASQUE SAUCE
RAPE EN CAZUELITA CON SALSA VASCA

MAKES 12 SERVINGS

⅓ cup olive or vegetable oil
1 clove garlic
1 teaspoon finely chopped fresh parsley
2 pounds monkfish, cut into 12 small fillets
salt
2 cups plus 2 heaping teaspoons all-purpose flour
1 cup boiling fish broth (page 181)
½ teaspoon turmeric

1. Heat the oil in a large skillet. Add the garlic, and sauté until golden. Remove the garlic with a slotted spoon, and place in a mortar with the parsley. Mash together, and reserve.

2. Cut the monkfish into 12 serving pieces, then season the fillets with salt to taste, and dredge in 2 cups flour. In the oil remaining in the skillet, sauté the fish for 1 minute on each side; do not let brown or cook through. Transfer the fillets to a heatproof earthenware or clay casserole, or a glass baking dish.

3. Add 2 teaspoons flour to the oil in the skillet, blending well over medium heat. Stir in the fish broth and the turmeric, and cook for 1 additional minute. Add the garlic-parsley mixture, and blend well.

4. Preheat the oven to 400°F. Pour the sauce over the fish. Cover the casserole with a tight-fitting lid or aluminum foil, and bake for 10 minutes. Remove from the oven, uncover, and serve.

MONKFISH IN ALMOND SAUCE
RAPE CON SALSA DE ALMENDRAS

A textural fish stew flavored richly yet subtly with ground almonds.

SERVES 8 TO 10

1 2-pound monkfish fillet
all-purpose flour
⅓ cup olive or vegetable oil
1 clove garlic
1 medium onion, finely chopped
½ pound tomatoes, seeded and diced
salt to taste
½ teaspoon sugar
24 almonds, blanched
1 teaspoon finely chopped fresh parsley
2 to 3 strands of saffron
1 egg, hard-boiled, chopped
3 tablespoons plus ½ cup water

1. Cut the monkfish fillet in half, and dredge each half in the flour. Set aside.

2. Heat the oil in a large skillet, and add the garlic. Place the fish in the hot oil with the garlic, and sauté until lightly browned. Remove the fish, and transfer to a baking dish. Remove the garlic with a slotted spoon, and place in a mortar. Set aside.

3. Place the onion in the remaining oil and sauté until transparent. Add the tomatoes, season with salt and sugar, and simmer over low heat about 5 minutes. Set aside.

4. Make a paste of the almonds, parsley, saffron, and sautéed garlic clove in the mortar and pestle, or puree in a food processor or blender. Stir in 3 tablespoons water. Add to the skillet containing the onions and tomatoes along with the remaining ½ cup water, and blend well. Bring to a boil over high heat.

5. Preheat the oven to 400°F. Pour the hot sauce over the fish. Cover with a tight-fitting lid or aluminum foil, and bake for 10 to 12 minutes. Remove from heat, uncover, garnish with the chopped egg, and serve.

VARIATION: Substitute 20 walnut halves for the almonds.

QUICK-FRIED MONKFISH
FILETES DE RAPE EMPANADOS

Delicious served on a bed of sautéed onions or layer of tomato sauce, heated through.

SERVES 8 TO 10

2 pounds monkfish fillets, pounded to ¼ inch thickness
salt
2 cups all-purpose flour
2 eggs
2 tablespoons plus 1 cup olive or vegetable oil
1 tablespoon cold water
freshly ground white pepper
2 cups fresh bread crumbs

1. Cut the monkfish into ½-ounce pieces. Season the fillets with salt to taste, if desired, and dredge in the flour. Set aside.

2. In a bowl beat together the eggs, 2 tablespoons oil, the water, and salt and pepper to taste. Dip the fish pieces in the egg mixture, then roll in the bread crumbs. Set aside.

3. Heat the remaining oil in a large skillet over high heat. Place one layer of fillets in the hot oil (the oil should just cover the fish pieces), and fry until crispy and golden. Remove, and drain on paper towels. Serve hot.

HAKE MORSELS SAN SEBASTIAN
COCOCHAS DE DONOSTIA

Donostia is the Basque name for the Cantabrian coastal city of San Sebas-
tian, and this recipe, made with two different kinds of hot peppers, lives up
to the region's fame for colorful, spicy, and sophisticated cuisine.

SERVES 4 TO 6

⅓ cup olive or vegetable oil
4 cloves garlic, 2 to 3 finely chopped
6–7 dried red peppers, seeded and pith removed (California or
    Pasilla peppers work well)
1 hot chili pepper, seeded
1 heaping tablespoon chopped fresh parsley
½ bay leaf
1 pound hake fillets cut into bite-size serving portions
all-purpose flour for dredging
1 tablespoon lemon juice
½ cup fish broth (page 181) or hot water
salt

1. Heat the oil in a large saucepan. Add 1 whole garlic clove and
sauté until golden. Add all the peppers, the parsley, the chopped
garlic, and bay leaf, and mix well. Dredge the hake fillets in the
flour, and add to the garlic-pepper mixture. Drizzle with the
lemon juice, and douse with the broth or hot water. Season with
salt to taste. Shake the saucepan to loosen any ingredients stuck
to the bottom. Cook the mixture over medium heat for 10 minutes, shaking the saucepan from time to time to prevent sticking.

2. Remove from heat, correct the seasonings, and serve.

HAKE MORSELS IN GREEN SAUCE
COCOCHAS O MEJILLAS EN SALSA VERDE

Cocochas, a great delicacy in the tapas bars of Basque country, are the flavorful, delicate "cheeks" of the hake, which are removed from the fish head and sold by weight. Bite-size morsels of hake fillet allow those of us without our own Basque fish monger to savor the following two preparations. Crisp steamed asparagus is an especially good garnish for this dish.

SERVES 8 TO 10

2 pounds hake fillets, cut into bite-size serving portions
all-purpose flour for dredging
⅔ cup olive or vegetable oil
4 large cloves garlic, finely chopped
1 heaping tablespoon chopped fresh parsley
1 bay leaf
1 cup fish broth (page 181) or water
salt

1. Dredge the hake in the flour.

2. Heat the oil in a large saucepan. Add the garlic and parsley, and sauté for half a minute. Immediately add the hake, stirring to coat the fish with the garlic and parsley. Add the bay leaf and douse the mixture with the broth or water. Season with salt to taste. Shake the saucepan to mix the ingredients without stirring. Cook over medium heat for 10 minutes, shaking the pan from time to time to prevent sticking. Remove from heat and serve.

FRESH SARDINES STUFFED WITH SPINACH AND MUSSELS
SARDINAS RELLENAS A LA VIGÜESA

A flavorful and delicate preparation for this commonly used Mediterranean fish. Flaky white meat clothes a light mussel and fresh spinach filling.

MAKES 18 SERVINGS

18 fresh sardines, cleaned (page 181)
1 pound small mussels, cleaned (page 181)
1 cup water
2 tablespoons olive or vegetable oil, plus more for coating
1 clove garlic, minced
2 ounces fresh spinach leaves, washed and shredded
salt and freshly ground black pepper to taste
pinch grated nutmeg
2 eggs, slightly beaten
1½ cups fresh bread crumbs

1. Spread each sardine open, pressing gently against the back, and slide out the bone. Set the fish aside.

2. Place the mussels and water in a covered saucepan over high heat. Cook 2 to 3 minutes, or until all the shells are opened. Remove from heat, and let cool in the cooking liquid. Remove the mussels from the saucepan and shell them, reserving 3 tablespoons of the broth.

3. Heat 2 tablespoons olive oil in a skillet. Add the garlic, and sauté until golden. Add the spinach, season with salt and pepper, and nutmeg, and sauté until the spinach is wilted. Add the mussels and reserved cooking liquid, and sauté for 2 minutes longer. Add the eggs, and stir to combine all the ingredients. Correct the seasonings, and remove from heat. Scrape the mixture into a bowl, and let cool.

4. Stuff each sardine with 1 teaspoon of the spinach-mussel filling, making sure to use at least 1 mussel per sardine.

5. Preheat the oven to 400°F, then lightly grease a large baking dish with oil.

6. Fill a small shallow bowl to ½ inch deep with olive oil. Dip each stuffed sardine in the oil to coat lightly and evenly, then roll the fish in the bread crumbs. Place the sardines in a single layer in the baking dish, and bake for 5 to 8 minutes, or until golden. Remove the sardines from the oven, cover, and let rest for 5 to 10 minutes before serving.

FRESH SARDINES IN TOMATO-SHERRY SAUCE
SARDINAS SEVILLANAS

SERVES 10 TO 12

24 fresh sardines, cleaned (page 181)
⅓ cup olive or vegetable oil
1 small clove garlic
1 bay leaf
1 medium onion, thinly sliced
½ pound tomatoes, peeled, seeded, and diced
salt to taste
pinch sugar
1 cup water
3 tablespoons manzanilla or other fruity white sherry (optional)
1 clove garlic and 2 to 3 strands of saffron ground together
1 tablespoon thinly sliced parsley sprigs

1. Place the sardines in a shallow baking dish, and set aside.

2. Heat the oil in a skillet. Add the garlic and bay leaf, and sauté until the garlic is golden. Add the onion, and sauté until transparent but not browned. Add the tomatoes, season with salt and sugar, and simmer over low heat for 10 minutes. Add the water and sherry. Stir in the garlic and saffron mixture. Correct the seasonings, and remove from heat.

3. Preheat the oven to 400°F. Place the sardines in a baking dish, then pour the sauce over them. Sprinkle with the parsley, and bake for 5 to 7 minutes, or until the fish is white at the thickest part. Remove from heat. May be served hot or cold.

SARDINE ROLLS OVIEDO WITH GREEN PEPPER SAUCE
ROLLITOS DE SARDINA A LA OVETENSE

Easy to make, these crispy sardine rolls can be prepared in advance up to the point of frying and are accompanied with a pepper sauce for dunking.

MAKES 24

12 fresh large sardines, cleaned (page 181)
1 large clove garlic, finely chopped
1 teaspoon finely chopped fresh parsley
½ teaspoon salt
½ teaspoon paprika
½ teaspoon lemon juice
2 tablespoons white wine
all-purpose flour for dredging
2 eggs, slightly beaten
1 cup fresh bread crumbs
oil for frying

1. Open each sardine and spread flat, pressing gently against the back. Remove the bones, and cut the fish in half lengthwise into 2 fillets. Rinse well, and pat dry. Place the fillets in a glass or stainless steel bowl, and set aside.

2. Combine the garlic, parsley, salt, paprika, lemon juice, and wine in a small bowl, and pour over the fish. Cover and marinate in the refrigerator for 1 hour.

3. Remove the sardines from the marinade, and dredge in the flour. Roll each fillet into a tight curl, and secure with a toothpick. Dip the curls in the egg, and roll in the bread crumbs to coat. Set aside.

4. Pour the oil into a skillet to ¼ inch deep, and heat. Fry the sardines in the hot oil until golden. Remove with a slotted spoon, and drain on paper towels. Arrange the fish on a serving dish, and serve either with Oviedo Sauce (below) or plain as a quick and easy finger food.

Oviedo Sauce:

3 tablespoons olive or vegetable oil
1 clove garlic, finely chopped
2 tablespoons finely chopped onion
½ teaspoon paprika
1 large sweet pepper, roasted (page 183), thinly sliced
3 tablespoons fish broth (page 181) or water
salt to taste
pinch sugar
1 teaspoon cornstarch
2 to 3 strands of saffron, crumbled
2 tablespoons cold water

1. Heat the oil in a small saucepan. Add the garlic and onion, and sauté until the onion is wilted. Stir in the paprika, blending well. Add the roasted pepper slices, then the broth or water. Season with salt and sugar, and simmer over low heat for 10 minutes. Remove from heat, and pour the sauce into a blender or food processor. Puree for 10 seconds at low speed. Return the puree to the saucepan, and set aside.

2. In a small bowl mix together the cornstarch and saffron. Add the cold water, and blend well to dilute the cornstarch. Stir into the puree. Place over medium heat, and cook for 1 minute longer. Pour the sauce into a serving dish and pass with the fish.

BARBECUED SARDINES STEAMED IN LETTUCE
SARDINAS ESPETILLAS

This recipe calls for briefly steaming freshly barbecued sardines in lettuce leaves, for extra juiciness. The lettuce "bundles" also make for easy serving and an attractive presentation.

SERVES 6 TO 8

1 pound fresh sardines, heads removed and cleaned (page 181)
salt to taste
olive oil
10 to 12 fresh lettuce leaves, rinsed and patted dry

1. Rinse the sardines under cold running water, and drain well.

2. Prepare the grill. Skewer 3 to 4 sardines on small skewers, season with salt, and drizzle with a small amount of olive oil. Grill the sardines over the hot coals, or on a hot kitchen grill, for 2 to 3 minutes on each side.

3. Remove the sardines from the skewers and wrap, 2 or 3 together, in the lettuce leaves. Let rest for 5 to 7 minutes, and serve.

NOTE: Marinating the sardines with coarse salt to cover in a shallow glass, stainless steel, or aluminum baking pan for 1 hour (refrigerated and covered) before cooking will also add extra juiciness.

SQUID IN BLACK SAUCE
RAJAS DE CALAMAR EN SU TINTA

SERVES 8 TO 10

4 pounds large squid, cleaned (page 181), with ink sacs
salt
1 cup olive or vegetable oil
2 cloves garlic, minced
½ pound onions, very finely chopped
½ pound tomatoes, peeled, seeded, and diced

1 tablespoon all-purpose flour
1 quart fish broth (page 181) or water
1 bouquet garni
freshly ground black pepper
dash grated nutmeg

1. Cut the tentacles and body of the squid into small serving pieces. Season the squid with salt to taste and set aside.

2. Heat ⅓ cup oil in a large saucepan. Add the whole garlic clove, and sauté until golden. Discard the garlic.

3. Add one-third to one-half of the squid at a time to the hot oil and sauté over high heat, adding more of the oil as needed. Cook for about 1 minute and not longer, so that the squid will not become rubbery. Do not let the squid brown. Remove with a slotted spoon, and transfer to a second saucepan.

4. Add any remaining oil to the oil in the skillet, and heat. Add the onions and minced garlic, and sauté until the onion is wilted. Add the tomatoes and sauté for 1 minute longer. Break the ink sacs open over the skillet, allowing the ink to drain into the tomato-onion mixture. Mix all the ingredients together well. Cover and sauté until all the juices are evaporated, 3 to 5 minutes. Stir in the flour, blending well, and slowly stir in the fish broth or water. Add a pinch of salt, and simmer over low heat for 10 minutes, stirring occasionally. Remove from heat.

5. Place a colander over the saucepan with the squid, and ladle the sauce into the colander, pressing with a spoon to force the sauce through. Add the bouquet garni to the squid. Place over very low heat, and cook for 30 minutes, stirring occasionally. Remove from heat. Correct salt, and season with pepper to taste and nutmeg. Serve immediately.

GOLDEN BATTER-FRIED SQUID
CALAMARES AL AMARILLO

SERVES 4 TO 6

2 pounds squid, cleaned (page 181)
salt
oil for frying
1 recipe fish batter or beer-flavored fish batter (page 176)

1. Cut the tentacles of the squid into bite-size pieces. Slice the body into thin rings. Season with salt to taste.

2. Pour the oil for frying into a large skillet to ½ inch deep, and heat. Dip the squid in the batter to coat, and drop the pieces in the hot oil. Fry until golden, remove from heat, and drain on paper towels. Serve hot.

OCTOPUS FOR A SAINT'S DAY FEAST
PULPO DE VERBENA

SERVES 4 TO 6

1 2-to-2½-pound octopus, cleaned
2 quarts cold water
salt to taste
1 bay leaf, or 1 bouquet garni
3 tablespoons olive or vegetable oil
2 cloves garlic
2 teaspoons paprika, or 1 teaspoon sweet paprika and 1
    teaspoon spicy paprika (available in specialty shops)
1 teaspoon all-purpose flour
⅔ cup broth from cooking the octopus
olive oil (optional)

1. Cut the octopus into bite-size pieces. Place the pieces in a saucepan with half the cold water and bring to a boil. Cook for 5 minutes, drain, and rinse under cold running water. Return the octopus to the pan and cover with the remaining cold water. Add salt to taste and the bay leaf or bouquet garni, bring to a boil, reduce heat, and simmer for 1 to 1½ hours, or until the octopus is tender. Remove from heat, and let cool in the cooking liquid. Drain, reserving ⅔ cup of the liquid. Set the octopus aside.

2. Heat the oil in a skillet. Add the garlic, and sauté until golden. Add the paprika, then the flour. Blend well, and quickly stir in the reserved broth from the octopus. Cook for 2 minutes longer to reduce the sauce. Remove from heat. Remove the garlic, and discard. Set aside.

3. Arrange the octopus in a serving dish. Pour the sauce over the octopus, and drizzle with olive oil, if desired. Serve.

CRISPY BREADED ANCHOVIES
BOQUERONES EMPANADOS

SERVES 4 TO 6

1 pound fresh anchovies, cleaned and without heads (see Note)
salt
flour for dredging
2 eggs, slightly beaten
2 cups fresh bread crumbs
⅓ cup olive or vegetable oil
1 lemon, thinly sliced

1. Spread each fish open by pressing against a hard surface along the bone. Remove the bone. Season the fish with salt to taste, and dredge in the flour. Dip the fish in the egg, then roll in the bread crumbs to coat.

2. Pour the oil to ¼ inch deep in a large skillet, and heat. Fry the fish, turning once, until golden. Remove from the skillet, and drain on paper towels. Serve hot, with thin slices of lemon.

NOTE: Fresh anchovies can be found in some parts of the East and West coasts. For a more readily available alternative, try fresh smelts.

FRIED EEL
ANGUILA FRITA

SERVES 4 TO 6

1 pound eel, cleaned, skin removed (page 180)
white wine
1 small onion, coarsely chopped
1 bouquet garni
salt
¼ teaspoon crushed white peppercorns
flour for dredging
oil for frying
2 eggs, slightly beaten

1. Cut the eel into 1½-inch pieces, then place in a large pot with white wine to cover. Add the onion, bouquet garni, salt to taste, and white pepper. Place over medium heat, bring to a simmer, and cook for 5 minutes. Remove from heat, and let the eel cool in the cooking liquid.

2. Remove the eel from the pot with a slotted spoon, draining well, and dredge in the flour. Pour the oil in a large skillet to ½ inch deep, and heat. Dip the eel in the egg to coat, then place in the hot oil, and fry until golden. Drain on paper towels. Serve hot.

VARIATION: For Breaded Fried Eel, after dipping the eel pieces in the egg, roll them in fresh bread crumbs to coat. Cook as above.

BARBECUED EEL ON SKEWERS
ANGUILAS ASADAS EN BROCHETAS

MAKES ABOUT 6 SERVINGS

1 pound eel, cleaned (page 180)
1 cup olive oil, plus more for cooking
1 bay leaf, crumbled
2 tablespoons finely chopped fresh parsley
2 tablespoons finely chopped onion
juice of 1 medium lemon
6 large fresh mushroom caps
1 cup tomato sauce (page 173) (optional)

1. Cut the eel into 6 bite-size pieces and place in a glass or stainless steel bowl. Add the oil, bay leaf, parsley, onion, and lemon juice. Toss well, and let marinate for 2 hours in the refrigerator.

2. Prepare a grill. Skewer 1 piece of eel and 1 mushroom cap on each of 6 skewers. Place on the hot barbecue or kitchen grill, and drizzle with olive oil. Cook for 2 to 3 minutes on each side, drizzling with more oil as needed. Remove from heat, and pull the eel and mushrooms off the skewers with a fork. Serve hot with heated tomato sauce, if desired.

SPICY GARLIC-SCENTED SHRIMP

GRILLED SHRIMP

COGNAC SHRIMP

GRILLED CLAMS

FISHERMAN'S STEAMED CLAMS

GYPSY CLAMS

SAFFRON CLAM AND POTATO STEW

CANTABRIAN-STYLE MUSSELS

MUSSELS WITH WILD MUSHROOMS

PORTUGUESE-STYLE MUSSELS WITH
TOMATO-PARSLEY SAUCE

CANARY ISLAND–STYLE MUSSELS WITH
TOMATO-COGNAC SAUCE

MUSSELS IN TARRAGON AND CAPER VINAIGRETTE

MUSSEL AND ONION STEW

MUSSELS IN GREEN SAUCE

5.

SHELLFISH TAPAS

GOLDEN BATTER-DIPPED MUSSELS

SNAILS WITH CHORIZO, ONION, AND GARLIC

SNAILS WITH LEEK, PEPPER, AND CHORIZO SAUCE SERVED ON
RIOJAN RICE

SNAILS SAUTÉED WITH ZUCCHINI AND TOMATO

SNAILS WITH MUSHROOMS

SNAILS IN GREEN SAUCE

COGULLADA ABBEY SNAILS

SNAILS WITH BURGUNDY BUTTER

FISHERMAN'S RICE

VINTNER'S-STYLE FRIED SNAILS

Like fish tapas, tapas based on shellfish are delectable, colorful, imaginative, and numerous. The many Mediterranean varieties of sweet rock mussels, tiny flavorful clams, shrimp, crayfish, crabs, and snails have inspired favorite recipes from everyone from fishermen newly arrived on the beach with a fresh catch to the haute cuisine chefs of Basque country. Likewise, their creations range from the simplest sprinkle of white wine, parsley, and saffron over steaming clams to a rich chorizo, leek, and red pepper snail sauce.

Largely bite-size, shellfish are a particularly adaptable finger food. Fried, grilled, or doused in a tangy sauce, they make fine appetizers to serve with any good dry sherry or wine.

Consult the Basics section for the best methods for preparing shellfish for cooking.

SPICY GARLIC-SCENTED SHRIMP
GAMBAS AL AJILLO

A classic.

SERVES 4

¼ cup olive or vegetable oil
1 clove garlic, finely chopped
½ to 1 whole dried chili pepper, seeded and thinly sliced
    (optional)
½ pound medium shrimp, shelled, deveined
½ teaspoon freshly ground black pepper
2 tablespoons water

Heat the oil in a large skillet. Add the garlic and chili pepper, and sauté for a few seconds. Stir in the shrimp and the black pepper. Add the water. Stir to combine, and cook for 3 to 5 minutes, or until the shrimp are bright pink. Remove from heat, and serve.

NOTE: The shrimp may also be grilled or barbecued, then tossed with the spicy garlic oil.

GRILLED SHRIMP
GAMBAS A LA PLANCHA

Refresh desired quantity of unshelled large shrimp under cold running water; drain well. Place the shrimp on a hot kitchen grill or griddle over hot flame or on a barbecue over aluminum foil. After 1 minute, turn the shrimp, and sprinkle with salt to taste. Grill for 1 more minute, remove from heat with a spatula, and serve. Scrape the grill clean with the spatula, and proceed as above with the next batch of shrimp.

COGNAC SHRIMP
CARABINEROS A LA AMERICANA

SERVES 12 TO 16

2 pounds large shrimp
2 jiggers of Cognac
⅓ cup white wine
½ cup olive or vegetable oil
1 clove garlic
1 heaping tablespoon finely chopped shallot
1 pound ripe, beefy tomatoes, chopped
1 teaspoon all-purpose flour
salt and freshly ground white pepper to taste
1 red chili pepper, seeded and chopped
1 cup water

1. Place the shrimp in a large pot. Douse them with the Cognac and white wine, and set aside.

2. Heat the oil in a skillet. Add the garlic, and sauté until golden. Add the shallot, and sauté until tender. Stir in the tomatoes, flour, salt, white pepper, and chili pepper. Cover, and simmer, stirring occasionally, until thickened. Add the water, and bring to a boil. Remove from heat.

3. Place a sieve over the pot containing the shrimp. Pour the sauce into the sieve, letting it drain onto the fish, making sure that all the fish is lightly covered with the strained sauce. Correct the seasonings of the sauce if desired, and place the pot over high heat. Bring to a boil, and simmer for 1 minute. Cover, and set the pot in a warm place until ready to serve.

GRILLED CLAMS
ALMEJAS A LA PLANCHA

SERVES 4 TO 6

2 pounds (2 dozen) medium clams, cleaned (page 180)
⅓ cup white wine vinegar
1 lemon, cut into wedges

1. Prepare a grill (you can use an outdoor barbecue covered with aluminum foil). Discard any clam shells that are broken or open.

2. Place the clams on the barbecue, a hot kitchen grill, or a pan-cake griddle over high flame, and cook until the shells open up. Drizzle a few drops of vinegar into each shell, and grill a few minutes longer. Remove from heat, and serve with lemon wedges.

FISHERMAN'S STEAMED CLAMS
ALMEJAS A LA MARINERA

Heaps of tender clams steeped in a garlic-wine sauce.

SERVES 4 TO 6

⅓ cup olive or vegetable oil
1 clove garlic, finely chopped
1 bay leaf
1 tablespoon finely chopped fresh parsley
1 tablespoon finely chopped onion
1 heaping teaspoon all-purpose flour
1 cup hot water or fish broth (page 181)
3 pounds (about 3 dozen) small clams, cleaned (page 180)
3 tablespoons white wine
salt and freshly ground black pepper

1. Pour the oil into a large saucepan and heat. Add the garlic, bay leaf, parsley, and onion, and sauté until the onion is transparent but not browned. Quickly whisk in the flour, stirring constantly to form a smooth sauce. Do not allow the mixture to brown. Slowly whisk in the hot water or broth, and bring to a boil.

2. Add the clams to the saucepan and toss with the garlic, onion, and herbs over high heat just to coat. Cover, and cook until all the shells are open, about 5 minutes. Pour the wine over the opened clams. Season to taste with salt and pepper, and remove from heat.

3. Remove the clams from the saucepan with the shells intact, and arrange in a serving dish. Cover the clams with the sauce, and serve.

VARIATIONS: Blend 1 heaping teaspoon tomato paste into the onion, garlic, bay leaf, and parsley mixture just before stirring in the flour.
  Substitute an equal quantity of mussels for the clams.

GYPSY CLAMS
ALMEJAS GITANAS

A coating of white sauce and bread crumbs makes these fried clams tender and succulent.

SERVES 4 TO 6

2 pounds (about 2 dozen) clams, cleaned (page 180)
½ cup manzanilla or other fruity white sherry
2 tablespoons butter
¼ cup all-purpose flour, plus extra for dredging
1⅓ cups milk
pinch of grated nutmeg
salt to taste
pinch freshly ground white pepper
2 eggs, slightly beaten
1 cup fresh bread crumbs
oil for frying

1. Place the clams in a pot with cold water to cover. Add the sherry and let macerate, refrigerated, for 1 hour. Cover the pot, place over high heat, and bring to a boil. When all the shells are open (2 to 3 minutes), remove from heat, and set aside to cool in the cooking liquid.

2. Melt the butter in a saucepan over low heat. Stir in the ¼ cup flour, stirring constantly to form a smooth paste. Slowly pour in the milk, whisking constantly, and cook until thickened. Remove from heat. Stir in the nutmeg, salt, and white pepper. Set aside until completely cooled.

3. Lightly grease a large platter, and set aside. Remove the cooled clams from their shells, and discard the shells. Dip each clam in the white sauce to cover, then dredge in the flour. Dip the clams in the egg to coat, then roll in the bread crumbs. Place the clams on the greased platter.

4. Pour the oil into a large skillet to ½ inch deep, and heat (the oil should be enough to just barely cover one layer of the clams). Fry the clams in the hot oil until golden. Remove with a slotted spoon, and drain on a paper towel. Serve hot.

SAFFRON CLAM AND POTATO STEW
GUISADILLO DE ALMEJAS CON PATATAS

SERVES 6 TO 8

2 pounds (about 2 dozen) medium clams, cleaned (page 180)
3 tablespoons olive or vegetable oil
2 tablespoons minced onion
pinch all-purpose flour
1 pound new potatoes, peeled
1 clove garlic, chopped, 1 teaspoon chopped
    fresh parsley, 2 to 3 strands of saffron, and
    6 toasted almonds mashed together
    in a mortar
salt and freshly ground black pepper
    to taste
pinch ground cinnamon
1 bouquet garni
finely chopped fresh parsley

1. Place the clams in a large saucepan with cold water to barely cover. Place over high heat, and bring to a boil. Remove from heat, and let cool in the cooking liquid. Drain the clams, straining the cooking liquid through a cheesecloth into a bowl. Reserve 2 cups of the liquid. Remove the clams from their shells, and discard the shells. Set aside.

2. Heat the oil in a large saucepan or *paellera*. Add the onion, and sauté until transparent but not browned. Stir in the flour, then slowly add 1 cup of the reserved clam broth. Add the potatoes and clams, combining well. Stir in the garlic, parsley, saffron, and almond mixture. Season with salt, pepper, cinnamon, and the bouquet garni. Simmer over low heat for 30 minutes, adding more of the cooking liquid if needed. Remove from heat and transfer to a serving dish. Garnish with the chopped parsley and serve.

CANTABRIAN-STYLE MUSSELS
MEJILLONES CANTABRICOS

SERVES 4 TO 6

¼ cup olive or vegetable oil
1 clove garlic
2 heaping tablespoons finely chopped onion
2 heaping tablespoons finely chopped carrot
½ teaspoon crushed red pepper
1 cup tomato sauce (page 173)
½ cup white wine
2 pounds mussels, cleaned (page 181)
½ cup finely chopped fresh parsley

1. Heat the oil in a large saucepan. Add the garlic, and sauté over low heat until tender. Remove the garlic, and discard. Add the onion and carrot, and sauté until the onion is transparent, stirring occasionally.

2. Stir in the red pepper, then add the tomato sauce and wine. Next, place the mussels in the saucepan, and cover. Let simmer over medium heat until all the shells are opened, 2 to 3 minutes.

3. Remove the mussels from the saucepan and remove from their shells, discarding the bottom half of each shell. Return the meat to the saucepan. Bring the mixture to a boil, and cook for 1 minute longer. Remove from heat.

4. Place 1 mussel in each shell half and spoon the sauce on top. Garnish with parsley, and serve.

MUSSELS WITH WILD MUSHROOMS
MEJILLONES A LA MADRILEÑA

SERVES 4 TO 6

2 pounds mussels, cleaned (page 181)
1 cup white wine (preferably Valdepeñas)
⅓ cup olive or vegetable oil
½ pound shiitake, porcini, or other wild mushroom of your
     choice, thinly sliced
2 cloves garlic, chopped
1 tablespoon finely chopped fresh parsley
1 tablespoon fresh bread crumbs
salt and freshly ground black pepper

1. Place the cleaned mussels in a large saucepan. Add the wine, cover, and place over high heat. Cook for 2 to 3 minutes, or until all the shells are opened. Remove from heat, and let cool. Remove the mussels from their shells, and reserve the meat. Discard the shells.

2. Heat the oil in a saucepan. Add the wild mushrooms, and sauté over medium heat, stirring constantly, until all the liquid released by the mushrooms evaporates. Add the mussels, tossing with the mushrooms to combine. Mix together the garlic and parsley, and add to the mussels. Stir all the ingredients to combine. Add the bread crumbs, and toss over heat until golden. Season with salt and pepper to taste, and serve.

NOTE: A few tablespoons of white sherry may be added at the end, if desired.

PORTUGUESE-STYLE MUSSELS WITH TOMATO-PARSLEY SAUCE
MEJILLONES PORTUGUESES

SERVES 4 TO 6

¼ cup olive or vegetable oil
1 clove garlic
1 cup finely chopped fresh parsley
2 pounds mussels, cleaned (page 181)
1 cup hot tomato sauce (page 173)

1. Heat the oil in a large saucepan. Add the garlic and half the parsley, and sauté for a few seconds. Add the mussels, and stir the mixture continuously until all the mussel shells are opened. Remove from heat.

2. Remove half the shell from each mussel, and discard. Arrange the remaining half-shells with the mussels attached on a serving platter. Pour the hot tomato sauce over the mussels, sprinkle with the remaining parsley, and serve.

CANARY ISLAND–STYLE MUSSELS WITH TOMATO-COGNAC SAUCE
MEJILLONES CANARIOS

SERVES 4 TO 6

2 pounds mussels, cleaned (page 181)
1 cup water
1 cup tomato sauce (page 173)
2 to 3 tablespoons Cognac, or to taste

1. Place the mussels in a large saucepan with the water. Cover and cook over high heat, 2 to 3 minutes, or until all the shells are opened. Remove from heat, and let cool.

2. Place the tomato sauce in a small saucepan with the Cognac. Stir to blend, and cook over medium heat until the sauce begins to boil. Set aside.

3. Remove the mussels from the saucepan. Remove half the shell from each mussel and discard, leaving each mussel attached or inserted in a half-shell. Arrange the mussels on a serving dish, and top each mussel with the Cognac-laced tomato sauce. Serve hot.

MUSSELS IN TARRAGON AND CAPER VINAIGRETTE
MEJILLONES SALSA VINAGRETA

SERVES 4 TO 6

2 pounds mussels, cleaned (page 181)
1 cup dry white wine
salt and freshly ground black pepper
3 tablespoons white wine vinegar
⅓ cup olive oil
pinch freshly ground white pepper
1 egg, hard-boiled, finely chopped
¼ cup finely chopped fresh parsley
1 tablespoon fresh tarragon leaves, or 1 teaspoon dried
1 tablespoon small capers

1. Place the mussels in a large saucepan. Add the wine, and season with salt and pepper to taste. Cover and cook for 2 to 3 minutes over high heat, or until all the shells are opened. Remove from heat and let cool. Remove 6 mussels from their shells, chop into small pieces, and set aside. Remove one-half of each shell from the remaining mussels, and place each mussel on a half-shell in a serving dish. Reserve the cooking liquid.

2. Pour the vinegar into a small bowl or measuring cup. Whisk in the oil in a slow steady stream until the mixture is emulsified. If too dense, add some of the reserved mussel and wine broth. Season with the white pepper, and add the chopped mussels. Pour the vinaigrette over the mussels in half-shells. Sprinkle with the chopped egg, parsley, tarragon, and capers, and serve.

MUSSEL AND ONION STEW
GUISADILLO DE MEJILLONES CON CEBOLLA

SERVES 4 TO 6

2 pounds large mussels, cleaned (page 181)
⅓ cup white wine
½ cup olive or vegetable oil
1 clove garlic
1 pound onions, thinly sliced
1 teaspoon all-purpose flour
1 cup water
1 clove garlic and 2 to 3 strands of saffron mashed together
salt and freshly ground black pepper

1. Place the mussels in a large saucepan. Add the wine. Cover, place over high heat, and cook until all the shells are opened, 2 to 3 minutes. Remove from heat, and let cool. Drain the cooking liquid, pouring it through a fine sieve, and reserve. Remove the mussels from their shells.

2. Heat the oil in a large skillet. Add the garlic clove and sauté until golden. Remove the garlic and discard. Add the onions to the skillet. Cover, and sauté until transparent and just beginning to brown. Stir in the flour, blending well. Add the water, bring to a simmer, and cook for 5 minutes. Add the reserved cooking liquid from the mussels, and the garlic-saffron mixture. Stir in the mussels, season with salt and pepper to taste, and cook for 2 minutes longer. Remove from heat and serve.

MUSSELS IN GREEN SAUCE
CAZUELA DE MEJILLONES EN SALSA VERDE

SERVES 4 TO 6

2 pounds mussels, cleaned (page 181)
4 cloves garlic, 2 finely chopped
1 cup finely chopped fresh parsley
3 tablespoons cold water
⅓ cup olive or vegetable oil
1 small hot red pepper, seeded (optional)
1 heaping teaspoon all-purpose flour
salt and freshly ground white pepper

1. Place the mussels in a saucepan with cold water to cover. Place over high heat. Just as the water begins to boil, remove from heat, and set aside. Let the mussels cool in the cooking water until they can be handled. Drain the liquid and reserve. Remove the mussels from their shells and set aside.

2. Mash the 2 whole garlic cloves and the parsley in a mortar. Add the 3 tablespoons water and blend into a thick paste. Set aside.

3. Heat the oil in a skillet. Add the chopped garlic, chili pepper, and the mussels, and stir. Blend in the flour. Do not let the mixture begin to brown. Add 1 cup of the reserved cooking liquid, then the garlic and parsley mixture. Season with salt and white pepper to taste, and stir to blend. Simmer for 2 to 3 minutes longer. Remove from heat and serve.

GOLDEN BATTER-DIPPED MUSSELS
COSITAS

MAKES ABOUT 24

¾ cup all-purpose flour, plus extra for dredging
1 heaping teaspoon baking powder
1 egg
1 tablespoon olive oil
½ teaspoon salt
freshly ground black pepper to taste
⅓ cup milk
2 pounds mussels, cleaned (page 181)
⅓ cup white wine
oil for frying

1. Prepare the frying batter: combine ¾ cup flour and the baking powder in a mixing bowl. Make a well in the center, and add the egg, 1 tablespoon olive oil, salt, pepper, and milk. Mix with rapid strokes until all the dry ingredients are moistened. Cover, and set aside for 10 minutes.

2. Place the mussels in a large saucepan with the wine and salt and pepper to taste. Cover, and bring to a boil over high heat. Reduce heat and cook for 2 to 3 minutes, or until all the shells are opened. Remove from heat, and let the mussels cool in the cooking liquid. Shell the mussels, dredge them in the flour, and set aside.

3. Pour oil into a large skillet to ½ inch deep, and heat. Dip the mussels in the frying batter to coat, and place them in the hot oil. Fry until golden. Remove the mussels from the skillet with a slotted spoon, drain on paper towels, and serve hot.

SNAILS WITH CHORIZO, ONION, AND GARLIC
CARACOLES A LA ANDALUZA

These Andalusian snails are even more delicious if prepared one day in advance, allowing the snails to marinate in the spicy sauce for a 24-hour period.

SERVES 4 TO 6

2 pounds large white snails, soaked (page 181)
1 large carrot, peeled
1 small onion studded with 2 cloves
1 bouquet garni

Sauce:
⅓ cup olive or vegetable oil
2 cloves garlic, minced
4 tablespoons thinly sliced onion
½ pound chorizo sausage, casing removed, very thinly sliced
1 heaping teaspoon paprika
1 heaping teaspoon all-purpose flour
2 cups chicken broth

1. Place the snails in a large pot with water to cover. Bring to a boil over high heat. Remove from heat, drain, and rinse under cold running water. Return the drained snails to the pot, and refill with water to cover. Add the carrot, clove-studded onion, and bouquet garni. Bring to a boil and simmer over low heat until tender, about 2 hours. Drain, discard the vegetables, and set the snails aside.

2. To prepare the sauce, heat the oil in a skillet. Add the garlic, sliced onion, and chorizo, and sauté until the onion is transparent. Stir in the paprika, then immediately stir in the flour. Blend well, and slowly whisk in the chicken broth. Let simmer for 10 minutes. Add the snails, and simmer for 10 minutes longer.

SNAILS WITH LEEK, PEPPER, AND CHORIZO SAUCE SERVED ON RIOJAN RICE
CARACOLES A LA RIOJANA

SERVES 4 TO 6

2 pounds large snails, soaked (page 000)
1 large carrot, peeled
1 small onion studded with 2 cloves
2 bouquets garnis
2 tablespoons butter, or 3 tablespoons olive oil
2 tablespoons all-purpose flour
⅓ cup water
1 leek, coarsely chopped
1 heaping tablespoon tomato paste or thick tomato sauce
2 tablespoons white wine
salt
pinch freshly ground white pepper
½ sweet red pepper, cored, seeded, and diced
¼ pound chorizo, thinly sliced
1 tablespoon olive oil

1. Cook the snails as for Snails with Chorizo, Onion, and Garlic (page 125). Drain, reserving the cooking liquid, and set aside.

2. Place the butter or oil and flour in a large saucepan, and place over medium heat. Stir until all the butter is melted and the mixture begins to brown. Add the water to the broth reserved from the snails, and slowly pour the combined liquids into the flour mixture, whisking constantly to prevent lumps from forming. Add 1 bouquet garni and the leek. Bring to a boil, and let simmer over moderate heat for 10 minutes. Add the tomato paste or sauce, white wine, salt to taste, and white pepper, blending well. Remove from heat, and pour the mixture through a colander or sieve into a large bowl.

3. Return the mixture to the saucepan. Add the snails, and bring to a boil over high heat. Let boil for 2 to 3 minutes. Remove from heat.

4. In a small bowl mix together the diced pepper and the chorizo slices. Add the tablespoon of olive oil, and toss to coat. Mix in with the snails. Serve the snails hot with Riojan Rice (below).

Riojan Rice:

2 cups water
2 tablespoons olive or vegetable oil
1 tablespoon minced onion
½ pound short-grain rice
salt
2 to 3 strands of saffron, crumbled
1 bouquet garni
1 tablespoon butter

1. Bring the water to boil in a saucepan.

2. In the meantime, heat the 2 tablespoons oil in a skillet. Add the onion, and sauté for 30 seconds. Add the rice. Mix together well so that all the rice grains become coated with the oil. Add the boiling water, season with salt to taste, and stir in the saffron and bouquet garni. Lower heat to a simmer, cover, and cook for 15 minutes.

3. Preheat the oven to 350° or 375°F. Transfer the rice to a baking pan, and bake for 15 minutes. Remove from the oven and stir in the butter.

SNAILS SAUTÉED WITH ZUCCHINI AND TOMATO
CARACOLES A LA ARAGONESA

SERVES 4 TO 6

2 pounds large snails, soaked (page 181)
1 large carrot, peeled
1 small onion studded with 2 cloves
1 bouquet garni

Pisto Sauce:
½ cup olive or vegetable oil
1 clove garlic
2 tablespoons finely chopped onion
1 pound tomatoes, chopped
2 zucchini, sliced into thin rounds
1 teaspoon paprika
salt and freshly ground black pepper
1 teaspoon finely chopped fresh parsley

1. Cook the snails as for Snails with Chorizo, Onion, and Garlic (page 125). Drain, and set aside.

2. To prepare the pisto sauce, heat the oil in a skillet. Add the garlic, onion, tomatoes, squash, paprika, salt and pepper to taste. Sauté over moderate heat for 2 to 3 minutes, or until the vegetables are crisp-tender.

3. Add the snails and parsley to the sauce, mixing well. Let simmer over low heat for 10 minutes. Remove from heat and serve.

SNAILS WITH MUSHROOMS
CARACOLES A LA SEVILLANA

SERVES 4 TO 6

2 pounds large snails, soaked (page 181)
1 large carrot, peeled
1 small onion studded with 2 cloves
1 bouquet garni
6 tablespoons olive or vegetable oil
1 clove garlic
2 heaping tablespoons finely chopped onion
1 heaping teaspoon finely chopped fresh parsley
2 heaping tablespoons tomato paste
½ pound mushrooms, cleaned and quartered
⅓ cup water or beef broth
pinch sugar
salt
3 tablespoons white wine
1 cup water
1 egg, hard-boiled, chopped (optional)

1. Cook the snails as for Snails with Chorizo, Onion, and Garlic (page 125). Drain, and set aside.

2. Heat 3 tablespoons oil (or use butter, if preferred) in a large saucepan. Add the garlic, and sauté until golden. Add the snails, stirring to coat with oil. Remove from heat, and reserve.

3. In another large saucepan heat the remaining 3 tablespoons oil. Add the onion and parsley. Sauté, covered, over low heat until the onion is transparent but not browned. Add the tomato paste, mushrooms, ⅓ cup water or broth, sugar, and salt to taste. Bring to a boil, and simmer for 2 minutes. Add the wine, and 1 cup water. Bring to a boil. Correct the seasonings, add the snails, and heat through. Remove from heat, and place the snails in a deep serving dish or platter. Sprinkle with chopped egg, if desired, and serve.

SNAILS IN GREEN SAUCE
CARACOLES EN SALSA VERDE A LA VASCA

This dish may be garnished with steamed asparagus tips.

SERVES 4 TO 6

2 pounds large snails, soaked (page 181)
1 large carrot, peeled
1 small onion studded with 2 cloves
1 bouquet garni
3 tablespoons olive or vegetable oil
2 cloves garlic
1 heaping teaspoon all-purpose flour
3 tablespoons water
1 heaping tablespoon finely chopped fresh parsley
3 tablespoons white wine
1 10-ounce package frozen green peas
salt and freshly ground black pepper

1. Cook the snails as for Snails with Chorizo, Onion, and Garlic (page 125). Drain, and set aside.

2. Heat the oil in a large skillet or saucepan. Add the garlic, and sauté until golden. Remove the garlic with a slotted spoon, and reserve. Stir the flour into the remaining oil to form a paste. Add the water and blend well. Remove from heat and set aside.

3. Place the reserved garlic and parsley in a mortar, and mash well until a paste is formed. Add the wine, and stir to blend. Add the paste to the flour mixture. Place over medium heat, and bring to a boil. Lower heat, and simmer for 15 minutes, stirring occasionally. Add the peas, and simmer for 3 minutes longer. Stir in the snails, season with salt and pepper to taste, and simmer for 2 more minutes. Remove from heat and serve.

COGULLADA ABBEY SNAILS
CARACOLES AL ESTILO DE LA ABADIA DE COGULLADA

SERVES 10 TO 12

50 large snails, soaked (page 181)
2 tablespoons butter
1 heaping tablespoon finely chopped onion
1 heaping tablespoon all-purpose flour
1 cup heavy cream
2 egg yolks slightly beaten with 2 tablespoons melted, cooled butter
salt to taste
pinch freshly ground white pepper
6 cups steamed white rice
½ cup chopped truffles or mushrooms

1. Place the snails in a large saucepan with cold water to cover and bring to a boil over high heat. Reduce heat and let simmer for about 2 hours. Remove from heat and let cool in the cooking liquid. Drain. Remove the snails from their shells with a toothpick or cocktail fork and cut off and discard the black end. Reserve the meat.

2. In a large saucepan melt the butter over medium heat, add the onion, and sauté until tender. Add the snail meat, then the flour, stirring constantly. Stir in the heavy cream and cook, stirring constantly, over low heat, for 10 minutes. Remove from heat. Add a few tablespoons of the sauce to the egg-butter mixture, blend, and return to the rest of the sauce. Season with salt and white pepper.

3. Spoon the steamed rice evenly around the outside edge of a large serving dish, forming a wreath (or use a ring mold to fit the outer edge of the dish). Spoon the snails into the center of the rice ring, forming a mound. Sprinkle with the truffles or mushrooms, and serve immediately.

SNAILS WITH BURGUNDY BUTTER
CARACOLES A LA BORGOÑESA

SERVES 4 TO 6

2 pounds large snails, soaked (page 181)
5 ounces carrots, peeled, quartered, and cut into thin strips
1 medium onion, coarsely sliced
1 stalk celery
1 bouquet garni
pinch cayenne
2 black peppercorns
pinch freshly ground white pepper
1 teaspoon salt (optional)
¼ cup fresh bread crumbs

Burgundy Butter:
2 heaping teaspoons finely chopped shallot
20 leaves fresh tarragon, washed, patted dry, and finely chopped
10 leaves fresh chervil, washed, patted dry, and finely chopped
2 small cloves garlic, finely chopped
1 heaping teaspoon finely chopped fresh parsley
pinch salt
3 sticks butter, softened at room temperature
freshly ground black pepper to taste
pinch grated nutmeg
pinch ground ginger
2 jiggers of Cognac

1. Place the snails in a large saucepan with cold water to cover. Place over high heat and bring to a boil. Remove from heat, drain, and rinse under cold running water. Drain well.

2. Return the snails to the saucepan and cover again with cold water. Add the carrots, onion, celery, bouquet garni, and seasonings. Bring to a boil over high heat, strain the foam from the top, reduce heat, and let simmer for 2 hours. Remove from heat, and let cool in the cooking liquid.

3. While the snails are cooling, prepare the burgundy butter. Place the shallot, tarragon, chervil, garlic, parsley, and salt in the bowl of a food processor or in a blender and chop until a fine paste is formed. Blend in the butter, a few tablespoons at a time to form a thick creamy spread. Season with pepper, nutmeg, and ginger. Slowly blend in the Cognac to obtain a smooth butter, taking care not to overdilute. Set aside.

4. Drain the snails and remove them from their shells with a toothpick or cocktail fork. Cut off the black ends and discard. Stuff each snail into a shell. Fill the ends of the shells with burgundy butter and place them on a serving platter. Sprinkle with bread crumbs and serve.

FISHERMAN'S RICE
ARROZ A LA MARINERA

Even rice can be served as a tapa, in small individual serving dishes. This dish is prepared with clams, mussels, eel, shrimp, monkfish, and freshwater or sea crabs. A full, flavorful classic, this is a seafood lover's dream—and very easy to prepare.

SERVES 4 to 6

1 quart plus 1 cup water
½ cup plus 2 tablespoons olive or vegetable oil
3 cloves garlic, 2 minced
1 heaping teaspoon finely chopped onion
2 tablespoons tomato paste
¾ pound shrimp, shelled and deveined (see Note)
½ pound eel (page 180), cut into bite-size pieces
½ pound monkfish fillets, cut into ½-ounce pieces
1 pound short-grain rice
½ pound clams or mussels, cleaned (pages 180 or 181)
2 sweet red peppers, roasted, (page 183), cut into thin strips
3 tablespoons frozen peas
4 to 5 strands of saffron
salt
12 small freshwater or sea crabs or crab legs, or 1½ cups
    crabmeat

1. Bring the water to a boil in a large saucepan. In the meantime, heat the oil in a paellera or large saucepan. Add the minced garlic and onion, and sauté until tender. Add the tomato paste, and mix well. Add the shrimp and the eel. Stir-fry for a few minutes over medium heat. Add the monkfish, mixing well. Stir in the rice, making sure that each grain is coated well with the oil. Pour in the boiling water. Add the clams or mussels, roasted peppers, and peas, and continue to simmer.

2. In a mortar mash together the whole clove of garlic, saffron, and 1 teaspoon salt. Add 3 tablespoons cold water, and stir to dissolve the salt. Add the mixture to the seafood. Season with more salt if desired, to taste, and cook for 5 minutes longer.

3. Preheat the oven to 375°F. Spoon the seafood mixture into a large baking dish or casserole. Cover and bake for 10 minutes. Remove the dish from the oven and mix well, making sure that all the ingredients are evenly distributed. Garnish the top of the rice dish with the crabs. Cover and return the dish to the oven, and bake for 5 to 6 minutes longer, or until the liquid is absorbed. Remove from the oven and let rest, covered, for a few minutes before serving.

NOTE: An equal quantity of prawns may be substituted for the shrimp, if desired.

VINTNER'S-STYLE FRIED SNAILS
CARACOLES (BUNUELOS) AL ESTILO DEL VIÑADOR

SERVES 10 TO 12

50 large snails, soaked (page 181)
oil for frying
1 clove garlic, finely chopped
1 cup finely chopped fresh parsley
3 tablespoons dry red wine
salt to taste
pinch freshly ground white pepper
⅓ cup vegetable shortening
2 scallions, finely chopped
1 cup all-purpose flour

1. Place the snails in a large saucepan with cold water to cover, and bring to a boil over high heat. Reduce heat, and let simmer for 2 hours. Remove from heat and let cool in cooking liquid. Drain. Remove the snails from their shells with a toothpick or cocktail fork and cut off and discard the black end. Reserve the meat.

2. Heat ⅓ cup oil in a large saucepan. Add the garlic and 1 heaping teaspoon parsley, and sauté over low heat. Add the snails, wine, salt, and pepper. Let simmer about 10 or 15 minutes, or until the wine has evaporated. Remove from heat and set aside.

3. Melt the vegetable shortening in a large skillet. Add the scallions, and sauté for 1 minute. Dredge the snails one by one in the flour and drop into the skillet. Fry until golden and drain on paper towels. Fry the remaining parsley in a small amount of oil and sprinkle over the snails, if desired. Serve hot.

6.

POULTRY AND MEAT TAPAS

In large quantities, any of the following recipes could become a main dish. But as tapas—in tiny cubes with savory sauces, stuffed with vegetables, or sliced in tiny fillets and grilled, baked, or fried—these chicken and meat dishes are mouth-watering snacks that taste as good as the meal to come.

Meat and poultry tapas are best served hot or at room temperature. Keep them warm in the oven and set them out just before serving. Stewed meat tapas and tapas in sauces are delicious

137

reheated the day after they are prepared, when the flavor of the sauces becomes more pronounced. For most of these dishes, portions should be small enough to be skewered easily with a toothpick or to be picked up easily between two fingers. Stewed meats or those laced with sauce or rice can be served in small plates with forks.

SPICY GARLIC-SCENTED CHICKEN
POLLO AL AJILLO

MAKES ABOUT 20

2 2-pound chickens, cut into small serving pieces, gizzards and
   necks reserved
1 bouquet garni
1 onion, coarsely chopped
1 quart water
oil for frying
2 cloves garlic, finely chopped
2 tablespoons sherry or white wine
1 teaspoon cornstarch

1. Cut the tips from the chicken wings and place them in a saucepan with the gizzards, necks, bouquet garni, and onion. Add the water. Cover and bring to a boil over high heat. Lower heat, and simmer for about 1 hour, or until the broth is reduced to 1 cup. Set aside.

2. Heat ⅓ cup oil in a large skillet. Add the whole clove of garlic and sauté for a few seconds. Add the chicken, 4 to 5 pieces at a time, and fry until golden on all sides. Add more oil as needed to fry all the chicken pieces. Drain the chicken on paper towels, then arrange the pieces in a large casserole or baking dish.

3. Preheat the oven to 375°F. Remove the garlic from the skillet and discard. Add the chopped garlic to the oil remaining in the skillet and sauté until lightly browned. Remove with a slotted spoon and sprinkle over the chicken pieces. Pour the sherry or wine and 3 tablespoons of the reserved chicken broth over the chicken. Place in the oven and bake for 5 to 10 minutes, or until the liquid begins to bubble. Bake for 25 minutes longer.

4. Meantime, return the remaining broth to the stovetop and cook until reduced to ⅓ cup. Stir in the cornstarch and continue to cook, stirring constantly, until thickened. Pour the sauce over the chicken, and bake the chicken for 5 minutes longer. Remove from heat and serve.

SPICY ALMOND-DIPPED FRIED CHICKEN
PANCHITAS CRIOLLAS

An almond, parsley, and garlic coating transforms southern fried chicken into a Mediterranean delight, a real surprise when you bite into it. Delicious with tomato wedges and sautéed zucchini or eggplant.

MAKES 6 TO 8 SERVINGS

24 toasted almonds (page 181)
1 clove garlic
1 tablespoon finely chopped fresh parsley
salt and freshly ground black pepper
1 1½-to-2-pound chicken, cut into small serving pieces
all-purpose flour for dredging
oil for frying
2 eggs, slightly beaten

1. Place the almonds, garlic, parsley, salt and pepper to taste in a mortar, and mash together.

2. Roll the chicken pieces in the mixture, then dredge in the flour. Set aside.

3. Pour the oil into a large skillet to ¼ inch deep, and heat. Dip the chicken pieces in the egg to coat, and fry in the hot oil until well browned and juice runs clear when the pieces are pierced with a fork.

VALENCIAN PAELLA WITH CHICKEN
PAELLA CON POLLO A LA VALENCIANA

MAKES 20 SERVINGS

½ cup olive or vegetable oil
2 chickens, cut into 10 serving pieces each
½ pound lean pork loin, cut into small cubes
½ pound eel, cut into 1-inch pieces (page 180), or ½ pound
    squid, cleaned (page 181), cut into small serving pieces, or
    ½ pound monkfish, cut into small serving pieces
2 plum tomatoes, peeled, seeded, and diced
1 pound short-grain rice
4 ounces peas, cooked
1 quart water
salt
1 small clove garlic and 3 to 4 strands of saffron mashed together

1. Heat the oil in a very large skillet or paellera. Place the
chicken pieces and pork in the hot oil, and sauté, stirring frequently, until well browned. Add the eel or squid (if using monkfish, bake or poach the fish separately, and add to the paella after
adding the saffron-garlic mixture, step 2), and sauté for 3 to 5
minutes.

2. Stir in the tomatoes and rice, stirring well to make sure all the
grains of rice are coated with the oil. Add the peas and the water.
Season with salt to taste, and add the garlic-saffron mixture.
Cook over high heat for 2 minutes. Reduce heat to medium,
cover and cook for 12 to 13 minutes longer, or until the liquid is
absorbed, and the rice is fluffy and tender. Remove from heat,
cover with aluminum foil or a lid, and let steam for 5 minutes
before serving.

VARIATIONS: Steamed shrimp, prawns, mussels, clams, or other shellfish,
and strips of roasted red bell pepper may be added after the rice has
cooked for 10 minutes.

STEWED LAMB WITH NEW POTATOES
GUISADO DE CORDERO CON PATATAS NUEVAS

SERVES 8 TO 10

2 pounds lamb cut into 1-inch cubes
salt to taste
pinch sugar
pinch freshly ground white pepper
3 tablespoons olive or vegetable oil
1 clove garlic
1 heaping tablespoon finely chopped onion
2 tablespoons all-purpose flour
1 pound tiny new potatoes, scrubbed clean
1 quart water
chopped fresh parsley

1. Place the lamb in a bowl. Add the salt, sugar, and white pepper, and toss.

2. Heat the oil in a large saucepan. Add the garlic, and sauté until golden. Remove the garlic with a slotted spoon, and discard. Add the lamb, and fry until browned. Remove with a slotted spoon, and place in a second saucepan.

3. Add the onion to the oil remaining in the saucepan, and sauté until tender. Stir in the flour, blending well. Add the potatoes, and toss to combine all the ingredients. Stir in the water, and bring to a boil. Remove from heat, and spoon the mixture over the lamb. Cover the saucepan, and cook over moderate heat for 45 to 50 minutes, stirring occasionally. Remove from heat, and place the meat in a serving dish. Garnish with parsley, and serve.

SPRING LAMB SONATA
SONATA DE CORDERILLO

This classic and excellent dish is prepared with kidney beans and Paschal Lamb.

SERVES 8 TO 10

2 pounds lamb shoulder
2 pounds white kidney beans in their pods
1 ham bone (see Note)
1 bouquet garni
1 medium carrot, peeled
3 tablespoons olive or vegetable oil
1 clove garlic, finely chopped
1 heaping teaspoon chopped onion
1 heaping teaspoon all-purpose flour
1 clove garlic, 1 tablespoon fresh parsley, and 2 to 3 strands of
    saffron, mashed together
salt and freshly ground black pepper
chopped fresh parsley for garnish

1. Cut the lamb in pieces about the size of hazelnuts. Set aside.

2. Shuck the beans, and place them in a very large saucepan with cold water to cover. Place over high heat, and when the water begins to boil, remove from heat and refresh under cold running water. Drain, and return the beans to the saucepan with cold water to barely cover over high heat. When the water begins to boil, add the ham bone, bouquet garni, and carrot. Reduce to a simmer.

3. Heat the oil in a skillet, and sauté the lamb over high heat until browned, stirring constantly. Remove the meat with a slotted spoon and add to the simmering beans. The beans and lamb should be just barely covered with water. Cover and cook over medium heat for 1 hour. Remove from heat, and set aside.

4. While the beans and lamb are simmering, reheat the skillet drippings and add the garlic and onion. Sauté until the onion is transparent but not browned. Whisk in the flour, blending well to prevent lumps. Cook over low heat, stirring constantly, for 10 minutes. Remove from heat, and press the mixture through a sieve into the pot containing the lamb and beans. Stir in the garlic, parsley, and saffron mixture, and cook over medium heat for 15 minutes. Season with salt and pepper to taste, and remove from heat. Discard the bouquet garni and reserve the carrot. Pour the meat and beans onto a serving platter. Garnish with slices of the cooked carrot and the chopped parsley and serve.

NOTE: If the ham bone is extra meaty, pick off the meat, chop into small pieces, and mash along with the garlic, parsley, and saffron mixture.

LAMB STEW BEJAR
EL CALDERILLO DE BEJAR

In Bejar, an old Castilian city in the province of Salamanca known for its fine hams, chorizo sausage, and centuries-old linen manufacturing industry, this specialty is quite popular.

SERVES 6

2 to 3 pounds lamb shoulder, cut into 18 pieces
salt and freshly ground black pepper
ground cinnamon
oil for frying
2 cloves garlic and 1 tablespoon chopped fresh parsley mashed
    together in a mortar to make a picada
1 heaping tablespoon all-purpose flour
3 tablespoons red wine
⅔ cup beef broth

Season the lamb with the salt, pepper, and cinnamon to taste. Pour the oil to ¼ inch deep in a large skillet, and heat. Brown the pieces of lamb well over high heat, stirring occasionally (the pieces should be slightly pink inside when done). Add the mashed garlic and parsley mixture. Stir in the flour, and quickly add the wine, then the broth. Cook for 1 minute longer. Remove from heat, and serve.

TENDER BÉCHAMEL-COATED LAMB CHOPS
CHULETAS A LA BÉCHAMEL

SERVES 8

2 pounds small lamb chops, some with bone, some without
3 tablespoons lard or vegetable oil
6½ tablespoons butter
1⅔ cups all-purpose flour
2 cups hot milk
salt and freshly ground black pepper to taste
pinch grated nutmeg
2 eggs, slightly beaten
1 cup fresh bread crumbs
oil for frying

1. Pound the chops with a meat pounder to ¼ inch to ⅓ inch thick.

2. Heat the lard or oil in a skillet and sauté the chops for about 5 minutes, or until cooked through but not dry. Set aside in a shallow bowl, letting the juices drain into the bottom of the bowl.

3. To prepare the white sauce (béchamel), melt the butter in a saucepan. Stir in ⅔ cup flour, forming a paste. Take care not to let the flour mixture turn brown. Slowly whisk in the milk, and bring to a boil. Add the juices from the lamb chops, and blend well. Simmer for 5 minutes longer over low heat, stirring occasionally. Remove from heat, and season with salt, pepper, and nutmeg.

4. Grease a large platter with a few drops of oil. Dip each lamb chop in the white sauce to coat. Place them on the greased platter, and let cool.

5. Pour oil for frying into a large skillet to ¼ inch deep, and heat. Dust the lamb chops with the remaining flour. Dip the chops in the egg, then coat with the bread crumbs. Place the chops in the hot oil, and fry until golden, about 1 minute on each side. Let drain on paper towels and serve hot.

BASQUE-STYLE STEWED PORK
CAZUELITA DE LOMO A LA VASCA

SERVES 8 TO 10

2 pounds lean boneless pork loin
salt and freshly ground white pepper
all-purpose flour for dredging
⅓ cup olive or vegetable oil
18 dried chili peppers
2 cloves garlic, minced
1 heaping teaspoon all-purpose flour
1 cup white wine
finely chopped fresh parsley

1. Slice the pork into bite-size ¼-inch-thick fillets. Pound with a meat pounder to ⅛ inch thick. Season on both sides with salt and white pepper to taste, and dredge the fillets in the flour.

2. Heat the oil in a large skillet. Sauté the fillets until very lightly browned on both sides. Remove from the skillet, and place in a baking dish or casserole.

3. Preheat the oven to 350°F. Add the chili peppers to the skillet, and sauté until softened but not browned. Add the garlic and flour, stirring to blend, cooking until the flour is lightly browned. Stir in the wine, blending well. Spoon the mixture over the pork. Cover the casserole with a lid or aluminum foil, and bake for 20 minutes. Remove, and let cool for 5 to 10 minutes. Garnish with parsley, and serve.

NOTE: If the sauce appears too dry, add a few tablespoons of beef broth before placing the casserole in the oven to bake.

CHUNGUITAS

Crispy and golden on the outside, hot melted cheese on the inside, and addictive.

MAKES 12 TO 15 LARGE PIECES

2 pounds lean boneless pork loin, cut into ¼"-thick 3"- × -4"
   slices
oil for frying
1 large onion, thinly sliced
½ pound Manchego, Gruyère, or other melting cheese, very
   thinly sliced
all-purpose flour for dredging
2 eggs, slightly beaten
1 to 2 cups fresh bread crumbs
lemon wedges and fresh parsley

1. Pound the pork slices to ⅛-inch thick. Set aside.

2. Heat 1 to 2 tablespoons oil in a skillet and sauté the onion until wilted. Place ½ tablespoon onion on half of the pork fillets, and spread evenly to the edges of each fillet. Place 1 slice of the cheese over the onions. Top with the remaining fillets to form sandwiches.

3. Dredge the meat sandwiches in the flour, dip in the egg to coat, then cover with the bread crumbs.

4. Pour oil to ½ inch deep in a large skillet and heat. Fry the sandwiches in the hot oil until golden and the juice runs clear when pierced with a fork. Remove, and let drain on paper towels. Serve the *chunguitas* with a garnish of lemon wedges and parsley.

NOTE: Large fillets may be cut in half to stretch this recipe to serve 24 to 30 bite-size pieces.

MALLORCAN VEAL CURLS
RIZOS DE MALLORCA

SERVES 12

12 2-ounce veal or pork loin cutlets
12 thin slices cooked ham, cut to size of veal or pork fillets
12 thin slices sobrasada sausage
all-purpose flour for dredging
2 cloves garlic
1 tablespoon finely chopped fresh parsley
1 bay leaf, crumbled
½ teaspoon dried thyme
1 teaspoon salt
½ teaspoon freshly ground black pepper
oil for frying
⅓ cup white wine
1 cup beef broth

1. Pound the veal or pork cutlets to ¼-inch thick. Top each with 1 slice of ham, then 1 slice of the sobrasada. Roll the fillets up tightly, and tie securely with kitchen twine. Dredge the curls in the flour, and set aside.

2. Place the garlic, parsley, bay leaf, thyme, salt, and pepper in a mortar, and mash together well. Reserve.

3. Preheat the oven to 350°F. Pour the oil into a saucepan to a depth of ¼ inch and heat. Add the mashed garlic, herb, and spice mixture to the oil, then the meat curls, and fry until the curls are browned, about 10 minutes. Transfer to a casserole or baking dish. Add the wine and cover. Bake for 5 to 6 minutes, or until the wine is evaporated. Add the broth, and bake for 20 minutes longer. Serve.

NOTE: This dish is best served with sautéed wild mushrooms (see p. 63).

HAM ROLLS WITH RED PEPPER AND MINCED PORK STUFFING
PEPILLOS

SERVES 6 TO 8

½ pound tomatoes, halved and seeded
1 pound medium potatoes, scrubbed clean
oil for frying
1 clove garlic
1 pound lean pork, chopped into chestnut-size pieces
salt
pinch sugar
3 large sweet red peppers, roasted (page 183) and coarsely
    chopped
3 tablespoons dry white wine (Cariñena, if available)
yolks of 2 hard-boiled eggs, 1 clove garlic, finely chopped, and 2
    tablespoons finely chopped fresh parsley, mashed together
2 to 4 tablespoons butter
¼ cup milk
½ pound Serrano ham, very thinly sliced
1 to 2 cups all-purpose flour
2 eggs, slightly beaten
2 cups fresh bread crumbs

1. Preheat the oven to 400°F.

2. Place the tomatoes in a baking dish, and bake for 10 to 15 minutes, or until soft. Chop into small pieces, and reserve.

3. Place the potatoes in a saucepan with water to cover. Bring to a boil, and simmer for 20 to 30 minutes, or until the potatoes can be pierced easily with a fork. Remove from heat, and let cool in the cooking water.

4. Heat 3 tablespoons oil in a skillet. Add the garlic and the pork. Fry until the pork nuggets are evenly browned. Add the tomato, and season with salt to taste and sugar. Add the roasted peppers, and toss to combine all the ingredients. Add the wine, and simmer until the wine is evaporated. Remove from heat, and let cool.

5. Grind cooled pork mixture coarsely in a meat grinder, place the mixture in a large bowl, adding the egg yolks mashed with garlic and parsley. Mix well and reserve.

6. Peel the cooked potatoes. Place them in a bowl with the butter and milk, and mash well. Set aside.

7. Spread the slices of Serrano ham on a table or countertop. Place 1 teaspoon of the pork filling at one end of each slice, and roll the slices up to form flute shapes about ½ inch in diameter, and 1½ inch long (you may have to slice the flute shapes in sections if the ham slices are wider than 1½ inch). Coat each roll with a ¼-inch layer of the mashed potatoes. Dust the rolls lightly with the flour and dip them in the beaten egg to coat. Roll the rolls in the bread crumbs to cover, and set aside.

8. Pour the oil for frying into a large skillet to ¼-inch deep, and heat. Fry the ham rolls in the hot oil for 5 to 8 minutes, or until golden. Drain on paper towels, and serve hot.

RABBIT BAKED IN SPICY SAUCE
CONEJO SALTEADO SALSA PICANTE

Serve with fried bread crumbs and steamed white rice, if desired.

MAKES 18 TO 20 SERVINGS

½ cup olive or vegetable oil
1 clove garlic
2 rabbits, cut into 9 to 10 serving pieces each, head and neck
  reserved
salt and freshly ground black pepper
1 medium onion, chopped
2 to 3 parsley stems, plus 1 teaspoon chopped fresh parsley
1 bay leaf
1 sprig fresh thyme, or ¼ teaspoon dried
2 heaping tablespoons all-purpose flour
1 cup water
⅓ cup white wine
1 tablespoon chopped shallot
1 tablespoon butter
freshly ground white pepper
pinch cayenne

1. Heat the oil in a large skillet. Add the garlic, and sauté for 1 minute. Season the rabbit with salt and black pepper to taste, and place, one layer at a time, in the hot oil. Sauté until well browned, 15 to 20 minutes, and transfer the meat to a large casserole or baking dish.

2. Preheat the oven to 375°F. Add the onion, parsley stems, bay leaf, and thyme to the skillet. Sauté until the onion is transparent. Stir in half of the flour, and cook until lightly browned. Stir in the water, and blend well. Remove from heat, and spoon the sauce over the rabbit pieces. Cover the casserole with a lid or aluminum foil, and bake for 45 minutes, or until the meat separates easily from the bone when tested.

3. Remove from oven, and skim the sauce from the pan through a sieve into a large measuring cup. It should measure about 1 cup. Pour the sauce into a small saucepan. If the sauce measured more than 1 cup, cook over low heat until reduced.

4. Place the wine and shallot in another small saucepan, and bring to a boil. Lower heat, and simmer for 5 minutes. Add the chopped parsley. Pour the wine mixture into the saucepan with the sauce, blending well. Set aside.

5. Melt the butter in a small skillet until soft, but not completely melted. Stir in the remaining flour, and blend well to form a paste. Set aside.

6. Place the rabbit sauce over high heat, and bring to a boil. Stir in the butter paste. Lower heat, and cook, stirring constantly, for 2 minutes. Season with white pepper to taste and cayenne. Correct the salt, if desired. Pour the sauce over the rabbit, and return the casserole to the oven. Bake until the sauce begins to bubble, about 2 minutes.

BASQUE-STYLE MEATBALLS WITH ASPARAGUS TIPS
ALBONDIGAS A LA VASCA

Exquisitely seasoned little balls of veal and pork are the centerpiece of this sophisticated tapa treat. A tomato sauce lightened with wine and spices clings to the succulent meat; the whole set off by crisp green asparagus tips.

MAKES ABOUT 36

½ pound asparagus
1 pound ground veal
½ pound lean ground pork
¾ cup fresh bread crumbs soaked in ⅓ cup milk
1 heart of lettuce, finely chopped
2 tablespoons finely chopped onion
1 egg
salt and freshly ground black pepper
all-purpose flour for dredging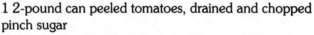
oil for frying
3 tablespoons white wine
1 clove garlic, finely chopped
1 2-pound can peeled tomatoes, drained and chopped
pinch sugar
1 clove garlic, 2 to 3 strands of saffron, and 1 heaping teaspoon
    finely chopped fresh parsley mashed together in a mortar

1. Cook the asparagus in boiling salted water until crisp-tender, 3 to 6 minutes. Remove from heat and drain, reserving 3 tablespoons of the cooking liquid. Plunge the asparagus immediately into a bowl of ice water and let cool. Drain well. Cut into 2-inch pieces, and set aside.

2. Combine the veal, pork, bread crumbs, lettuce, half the onion, egg, and salt and pepper to taste in a large bowl and mix well. With a tablespoon, measure out portions of the mixture about the size of a large walnut, and form into balls. Dredge the meatballs in the flour, shaking off any excess, and set aside.

3. Pour the oil into a large skillet to ¼ inch deep, and heat. Fry the meatballs in the hot oil until evenly browned. (Place only one layer of meatballs in the skillet at a time, and add more oil as needed.) Drain the meatballs on paper towels, place in a casserole or baking dish, and set aside.

4. In the remaining oil used to fry the meatballs sauté the other half of the onion until golden. Add the reserved cooking liquid from the asparagus, and the white wine. Mix well, and pour over the meatballs.

5. Preheat the oven to 350°F. Heat 3 tablespoons oil in a clean skillet. Add the garlic and sauté until golden. Add the tomatoes and sauté for 10 minutes. Season with salt to taste and the sugar. Pour the sauce over the meatballs. Cover the casserole with a lid or aluminum foil, and place in the oven. Bake for 30 minutes.

6. Remove the casserole from the oven and stir in the mashed garlic, saffron, and parsley mixture and the asparagus. Return to the oven, and bake for 5 minutes longer. Remove and serve.

SAUTÉED SWEETBREADS WITH GARLIC AND ONION
CAZUELITA DE MOLLEJAS SALTEADAS

SERVES 10 TO 12

2½ pounds calf sweetbreads
⅓ cup olive or vegetable oil
1 clove garlic
½ pound onions, thinly sliced
1 heaping tablespoon all-purpose flour
salt and freshly ground black pepper

1. Rinse the sweetbreads in several changes of cold water until the water runs clear. Place the sweetbreads in a large saucepan with cold water to cover. Cook over high heat until the water begins to boil. Remove from heat immediately, and drain. Rinse the sweetbreads under cold running water and drain well. Place a cloth or dish towel on a flat dish or tray. Spread the sweetbreads out on the cloth, a few inches apart. Fold the cloth over them (or use a second cloth) to cover. Place a flat weight (a cutting board will do) on top of the sweetbreads. Place a 2-pound weight on top of the cutting board. Refrigerate this way for several hours or overnight. Remove the sweetbreads from the refrigerator and slice in thin strips. Set aside.

2. Heat the oil in a large skillet. Add the garlic, and sauté until golden. Add the onion. Cover, and sauté over low heat until the onion is transparent but not browned. Add the pressed sweetbreads, mixing well with the onions and garlic. Stir in the flour, and cook, stirring rapidly, until all the ingredients are golden. Season with salt and pepper to taste, and serve.

GRILLED CALF'S LIVER WITH ROASTED RED PEPPER
BISTELITOS DE HIGADO CON PIMIENTOS

MAKES 50 PIECES

2 pounds calf liver, sliced into 50 tiny fillets
salt and freshly ground black pepper
½ cup olive oil
1 sweet red pepper, roasted (page 183), cut into thin slices

1. Prepare the grill. Season the liver with salt and pepper to taste. Dip the tiny fillets in the oil to coat. Place them on the grill or barbecue (if using a grill with grates, cover with foil and place the liver on top), or directly under the oven broiler, and cook until browned on both sides. Do not overcook because the liver will become dry.

2. Arrange grilled fillets in a serving dish. Decorate with pepper slices, and serve.

LIVER AND BACON ROLLS
CASTIZOS

MAKES 32

1 pound calf's liver, sliced into 32 ½-ounce fillets
16 strips bacon, cut in half
all-purpose flour for dredging
⅓ cup olive or vegetable oil
1 small onion, finely chopped
2 to 3 strands of saffron, 1 clove garlic, 1 teaspoon finely
  chopped fresh parsley mashed together in a mortar
⅓ cup beef broth or water
salt and freshly ground black pepper

1. Wrap each liver fillet with 1 piece of bacon. Dredge the rolls in the flour, and set aside.

2. Pour the oil into a large skillet, and heat. Place the liver-bacon rolls in the hot oil, and fry for 1 to 2 minutes, turning to cook evenly, until the bacon is browned. Do not overcook. Remove the liver with a slotted spoon, and drain on paper towels.

3. Sauté the onion in the oil remaining in the skillet until wilted. Add the saffron, garlic, and parsley paste to the sautéed onion. Stir in the beef broth or water, and season with salt and pepper to taste. Heat through just until bubbly. Pour the sauce over the liver-bacon rolls, and serve immediately.

SLICED CALF'S LIVER IN ALMOND SAUCE
FILETES DE HIGADO CON SALSA DE ALMENDRAS

MAKES ABOUT 50

2 pounds calf's liver, sliced into about 50 small fillets
salt and freshly ground black pepper
all-purpose flour for dredging, plus 1 heaping tablespoon
2 ounces shelled almonds, blanched
3 cloves garlic, finely chopped
3 to 4 strands of saffron dissolved in ⅓ cup water
⅓ cup olive or vegetable oil
2 cups hot beef broth
chopped fresh parsley

1. Season the liver fillets with salt and pepper to taste, and dredge in the flour. Set aside.

2. Place the almonds and whole garlic clove in a mortar, and mash together. Add the dissolved saffron to the almond and garlic mixture. Set aside.

3. Heat the oil in a large skillet. Fry the liver fillets in the hot oil 1 or 2 minutes, until golden on both sides. Remove from the skillet, and transfer to a serving dish. Sauté the chopped garlic in the remaining oil (add more oil if needed) for a few seconds. Stir in the 1 tablespoon flour, blending well. Stir in the beef broth, and season with salt and pepper to taste. Add the mashed almond, garlic, and saffron mixture, mixing well. Cook for 15 minutes over medium heat. Correct the seasonings. Pour the sauce over the fillets, sprinkle with chopped parsley, and serve.

VARIATION: Substitute 24 slightly toasted walnuts for the almonds.

BREADED LIVER FILLETS WITH STRAW POTATOES
FILETES DE HIGADO EMPANADOS CON PATATAS FRITAS PAJA

MAKES ABOUT 50

2 pounds calf's liver, sliced into 50 very thin fillets
salt and freshly ground white pepper
2 cups all-purpose flour
2 eggs, slightly beaten
2 tablespoons olive oil
1 tablespoon water
2 cups fresh bread crumbs
oil for frying

1. Season the liver fillets with salt and white pepper to taste. Dust the fillets with the flour, and reserve.

2. In a bowl beat the eggs with the 2 tablespoons olive oil, water, and a pinch each of salt and white pepper. Dip the floured fillets into the egg mixture, then roll them in the bread crumbs. Reserve.

3. Pour the oil for frying into a large skillet to ¼ inch deep, and heat. Fry the liver fillets in the hot oil, turning once, until golden. Remove, and drain on paper towels. Serve hot with Straw Potatoes (below).

Straw Potatoes:
2 pounds large potatoes, peeled
oil for frying
salt (optional)

1. Slice the potatoes lengthwise into ¼-inch-thick slices. Slice each round lengthwise into ¼-inch-thick strawlike strips. Place the potato straws in a large bowl with cold water to cover, and let soak for 1 hour. Drain the potatoes well, and pat dry with a paper towel.

2. Pour the oil for frying into a large skillet to ½ inch deep, and heat. Add the potatoes to the oil, small quantities at a time, and fry until golden. Remove with a slotted spoon, and let drain on paper towels. The potatoes may be kept warm in a preheated warm oven until ready to serve. Season with salt, if desired, just before serving.

NOTE: Once fried, these potatoes can be kept for several days without losing their taste by storing, rolled up in a cloth or dish towel, in the refrigerator. To serve, simply reheat them in a hot oven, and season with salt, if desired.

KIDNEY KEBOBS IN SPICY TOMATO SAUCE
PUNTILLAS

MAKES 24

Kebobs:

1 medium potato, peeled, or 12 thin raw asparagus tips, cut into
   thirds
12 beef kidneys, halved
24 wild mushrooms, washed, destemmed
salt and freshly ground black pepper
oil for frying
all-purpose flour for dredging
2 eggs, slightly beaten

Spicy Sauce:

⅓ cup olive or vegetable oil
2 cloves garlic, finely chopped
1 tablespoon all-purpose flour
2 tablespoons white wine vinegar
1 cup water
salt and freshly ground black pepper
onion salt
2 tablespoons tomato sauce (page 173) or canned
1 chili pepper, seeded, and thinly sliced

1. Slice the potato in half lengthwise. Slice each half in half lengthwise. Slice each section into 6 to 8 ¼-inch-thick pieces (about 24 to 32 pieces).

2. Skewer each kidney half and 1 potato slice on a thin wooden skewer. Skewer 2 wild mushroom caps next to the kidney. Season with salt and pepper to taste.

3. Pour the oil for frying into a large skillet to ¼ inch deep, and heat. Dredge the tiny kebobs in the flour, and dip in the egg to coat. Fry them in the hot oil until browned on all sides, 5 to 7 minutes. Remove from the skillet, and place in a glass casserole or baking dish. Keep warm in a 150° to 250°F oven while preparing the sauce.

4. Heat the olive oil in a skillet. Add the garlic, and sauté a few seconds only. Stir in the flour, blending well, and let brown slightly. Stir in the vinegar and water. Season with salt, pepper, and onion salt to taste.

5. Remove the kebobs from the oven. Ladle the mixture through a colander over the dish containing the tiny kebobs, and raise the oven heat to 400°F. Spoon the tomato sauce and chili pepper into the colander after the sauce, and press through onto the kebobs. Heat the kebobs for 2 minutes. Remove, and serve hot.

STEWED TRIPE WITH HAM AND CHORIZO
CALLOS A LA MADRILEÑA

A hearty tapa that can also be served as a main course, and even tastier the day after it is prepared.

SERVES 8 TO 10

Tripe:

2 pounds tripe, cleaned and diced
2 pounds calf's feet, cleaned, and split in half
6 ounces carrots
1 medium onion studded with 2 black peppercorns
1 celery stalk
1 small head garlic
1 bouquet garni
salt to taste

Tripe Sauce:

½ cup olive or vegetable oil
2 cloves garlic, chopped
4 ounces cooked ham, diced
4 ounces chorizo sausage, thinly sliced
1 medium onion, finely chopped
1 bay leaf
1 heaping teaspoon spicy (hot) paprika (available in specialty
    shops, or use regular paprika)
2 heaping tablespoons all-purpose flour
2 cups tripe cooking liquid
salt
1 teaspoon sugar

1. Place the tripe and calf's feet in a large saucepan with cold water to cover. Place over high heat. Add the remaining ingredients, and bring to a boil. Skim off any foam that comes to the surface. Cover, and simmer for about 3 hours, or until the tripe is tender. Remove from heat, let cool, and refrigerate, reserving the cooking liquid.

2. Heat the oil in a large saucepan. Add the garlic, ham, and chorizo, and mix well. Add the onion and bay leaf, cover, and sauté until the onion is transparent. Stir in the paprika, then the flour, blending well. Remove the tripe from the refrigerator. Stir the 2 cups cooking liquid from the tripe into the sauce, followed by the cooked meat. Bring to a boil, correct the salt, and add the sugar. Remove from the stovetop.

3. Preheat the oven to 350°F. Transfer the mixture to a casserole or baking dish. Bake, uncovered, for about 30 minutes. Remove, and serve hot.

7.

SPANISH OMELETTE WITH ALMOND SAUCE
EGGS STUFFED WITH FOIE GRAS
HARD-BOILED EGG SLICES
IN GREEN SAUCE COLMADO
STUFFED EGGS
EGGS MADRID

EGG AND CHEESE TAPAS

Few tapas are more well-known than those made from the simple egg. Stuffed, sauced, or coddled, eggs are versatile, quite readily available, and appealing to almost every palate.

The Spanish omelette (tortilla Española) is probably the best known of all tapas for Spaniards and foreigners alike. Made with tender potatoes and onions, it is delicious hot or cold. Practice makes perfect with the tortilla. Do not be fooled by its simplicity. The perfect Spanish omelette should be quite thick, the potato tender but not browned, and the center of the omelette ever so slightly runny.

Tapas made with boiled eggs are also popular. Tradition has it that the boiling egg is ready to be eaten after three *Paternosters* have been said; the chef of Philip II advised in a cookbook that if the cook has no hourglass with which to time his egg, he can instead say one *Pater*, one *Ave Maria*, and one *Salve*. (The untraditional can, of course, rely on the usual modern methods.)

Omelettes and other egg tapas are well suited for any occasion. They can be prepared well in advance or at the very last minute, a quality which makes them quite appealing to the busy or spur-of-the-moment host or hostess.

164

SPANISH OMELETTE WITH ALMOND SAUCE
TORTILLA ESPAÑOLA

One of the most familiar and beloved of tapas, this plump golden omelette sits atop almost every tapas bar. Unlike French-style omelettes, in Spain filling ingredients are mixed with the eggs, and approximately equal portions of each make for a dense, satisfying omelette that is sliced and served like a cake. It is best served warm or at room temperature and may be accompanied by Almond Sauce for a more unusual and festive touch. If you opt for Almond Sauce, you can make two small tortillas instead of one larger one, if you wish; spread each layer with sauce, and stack them. In this case, be sure to use a small frying pan to ensure that the omelettes retain their classic plump shape.

Tortilla:

½ cup olive oil
1 clove garlic
2 pounds potatoes, peeled, quartered lengthwise, and sliced into
⅛-inch slices widthwise (quarter-circle shapes)
1 medium onion, thinly sliced
Salt to taste
6 eggs, well beaten

Almond Sauce:

1 clove garlic, peeled and mashed in a press
¼ cup almonds, toasted (approx. 2 oz.) (see page 18)
1 teaspoon fresh parsley leaves, chopped
Few stems saffron
2 tablespoons dry white wine
2 tablespoons olive oil
1 teaspoon flour
1 cup chicken or beef broth
Salt to taste

1. Heat the oil in a large (9″) skillet. Add the garlic, and sauté until golden. Remove the garlic with a slotted spoon and discard. Add the potatoes and onion to the skillet, season with salt, and cook over low heat, covered, until potatoes are tender but not browned. This should take about 15 minutes. Remove from heat. Remove the potatoes from the skillet with a slotted spoon, draining well, and mix with the eggs in a large bowl. Make sure all the potatoes are coated with the egg, and add more salt if desired.

2. Place the skillet over high heat once more. Add more oil if needed just to coat the bottom. When the oil begins to bubble place the potato-egg mixture in the skillet, spreading evenly to cover the bottom and sides. Level the potatoes down with a fork. Lower heat, and cook until the egg on sides and bottom of the omelette begins to brown. Place a plate over the skillet to cover. Grip the skillet firmly with one hand, and place the second hand securely over the plate. Turn the skillet upside-down, flipping the half-cooked omelette onto the plate (it is best to do this over a sink to prevent spills). Quickly return the skillet to the stove, and slide the omelette, runny side down, back into the skillet. Cook until golden, but not overdone (an authentic Spanish Omelette is slightly runny on the inside). Flip the omelette onto a plate, and serve hot or cold. If you opt for Almond Sauce, it can be served in a sauceboat on the side, poured over the top, or, alternatively, once the cooked tortilla has rested a little, it can be baked in an ovenproof dish with a covering of Almond Sauce for 10 minutes in a preheated 325°F oven. In this case, let the baked tortilla cool slightly before serving.

To make Almond Sauce:

1. Make a picada of all the ingredients but the oil, flour, broth and salt: Place the mashed garlic in the mortar, add the almonds, and make a paste. Add the parsley and saffron, and mash again until the saffron is evenly mixed in with the other ingredients. Slowly stir in the wine and continue stirring until the paste is smooth.

2. In a sauté pan, heat the oil over low heat until it is warm but not hot. Add the flour, stir until it begins to take on color, about 30 seconds to 1 minute, then add the picada, followed by the broth. Add salt to taste, stir until the ingredients are evenly blended, and serve hot.

EGGS STUFFED WITH FOIE GRAS
HUEVOS RELLENOS DE FOIE GRAS

SERVES 12

6 large eggs, hard-boiled, shelled
6 ounces foie gras
1½ tablespoons butter, softened at room temperature
salt and freshly ground black pepper
1 tablespoon sherry
all-purpose flour for dusting
2 eggs, slightly beaten
1 to 2 cups fresh bread crumbs
⅓ cup olive or vegetable oil

1. Cut the hard-boiled eggs in half lengthwise. Remove the yolks and place them in the bowl of a food processor or in a mixing bowl. Reserve the whites.

2. Add the foie gras and butter to the yolks and season with salt and pepper to taste. Mix in the sherry and blend the mixture in the food processor (or mash together well with a fork in the mixing bowl) until a paste is formed.

3. Carefully stuff the egg whites with the egg–foie gras filling (you may choose to use a pastry sleeve with a decorative tip for a special effect).

4. Dust each stuffed egg half with the flour, then coat in the beaten eggs, and roll in the bread crumbs. Repeat this step, if desired, for a moister taste.

5. Heat the oil in a large skillet. Fry the egg halves in the oil until golden, about 1 to 2 minutes, turning to cook evenly all around. Drain on paper towels. Serve at once.

HARD-BOILED EGG SLICES IN GREEN SAUCE COLMADO
LONCHAS DE HUEVO DURO CON SALSA VERDE

MAKES 20 SERVINGS

2 cups fish broth (page 181) made with hake
oil for frying
2 cloves garlic
1 bay leaf
1 medium onion, finely chopped
1 tablespoon finely chopped fresh parsley
1 heaping tablespoon all-purpose flour
⅓ cup dry white wine
salt and freshly ground black pepper
5 slices of crusty bread, cut into 4 squares each
4 eggs, hard-boiled, cut into 5 slices each

1. Strain the fish broth, reserving the fish heads. Pick the meat from the fish bones, and chop fine. Reserve the meat, and discard the bones. Set the broth aside.

2. Heat ⅔ cup oil in a large skillet. Add the garlic and bay leaf, and sauté until golden. Remove from heat. Remove the garlic and bay leaf from the oil with a slotted spoon, and reserve. Add the onion and half the parsley to the oil, and sauté until the onion is transparent but not browned. Stir in the flour, blending well. Add the wine, and cook until evaporated. Add the fish broth and reserved bay leaf. Season with salt and pepper to taste. Place the reserved garlic and remaining parsley in a mortar, mash together, and add to the sauce. Cook for 10 minutes longer, until somewhat thick, and remove from heat.

3. In another skillet heat some oil and fry the bread squares. Place on paper towels.

4. Place 1 egg slice on each square of fried bread. Arrange the squares on a serving platter. Spoon the hot green sauce on top, and serve.

STUFFED EGGS
HUEVOS RELLENOS

1. Cook the desired quantity of eggs in boiling water to cover for 10 minutes. Remove from heat, and douse under cold running water. Crack the shells on a hard surface, and roll them between the palms of your hand to loosen the thin skin inside. Peel off the shells. Slice the eggs in half lengthwise, gently scoop out the yolks, and place in a bowl.

2. Stuff the whites with any of the following fillings:
marinated tuna (page 182)
tuna sautéed in olive oil with chopped tomato
pureed anchovies
anchovies and strips of roasted sweet red pepper (page 183), brushed with olive oil
pieces of steamed shellfish dabbed with homemade mayonnaise (page 172)

3. Mash the reserved yolks with a fork, and sprinkle over the stuffed eggs as a garnish, or add the yolks to the filling, and garnish the stuffed eggs with finely chopped fresh parsley.

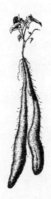

EGGS MADRID
HUEVOS CAFEFENÍA

In this spectacular preparation, eggs are shirred inside hollowed English muffins, blanketed with ham, and napped in an elegant mushroom wine sauce. Colorful, rich, and delicious, this dish is perfect for the most festive tapas occasion, yet it's easy enough to prepare that you may find yourself whipping up double servings for impromptu weekend brunches. If you wish, you can prepare the sauce in advance.

SERVES 6 AS A TAPA OR 3 FOR BRUNCH

Eggs:

6 English muffins or 1½-inch-thick slices of dense, crusty white bread
¼ cup olive or vegetable oil
4 tablespoons butter
6 eggs
6 slices of ham or cooked Canadian bacon
freshly ground black pepper

Mushroom Wine Sauce:

1 cup beef broth
1 heaping teaspoon cornstarch dissolved in 2 tablespoons dry sherry
4 tablespoons butter
¼ cup dry white wine or vermouth
2 tablespoons olive or vegetable oil
1 small shallot, finely diced
2 cups diced mushrooms (½ pound)
1 teaspoon all-purpose flour

1. Preheat the oven to 450°F. Grease a cookie sheet and set aside.

2. With a small sharp knife (a grapefruit knife works well), cut round "wells" into the whole English muffins or the bread slices to half the depth of the bread and to within an inch of the edges, taking care not to puncture the bottoms or sides. Set aside.

3. To prepare the mushroom wine sauce, bring the beef broth to a boil in a small saucepan. Whisk the dissolved cornstarch into the broth. Boil for 1 minute longer, or until the liquid thickens slightly. Pour the broth into a small bowl and reserve. In the same saucepan, melt 2 tablespoons butter over low heat. Add the white wine or vermouth. Add the ham or bacon slices and heat them in the liquid until warmed through, about 5 minutes. Reserve the meat. Stir the broth reduction into the wine, butter, and ham juices. Simmer for a minute until the flavors mix, and set aside. Heat the oil in a skillet over medium flame. Swirl in 2 tablespoons butter. Add the shallot, and sauté for 1 or 2 minutes, or until wilted. Stir in the mushrooms and sauté until they just start to render their juices, about 2 minutes more. Add the flour and stir to coat. Stir in the meats, sherry, butter, and wine mixture and simmer gently for 5 minutes. Keep the sauce covered on very low heat until the eggs are ready to serve.

4. Heat the oil in a large skillet and swirl in the butter. Fry the muffins or bread, "well" side down, until golden, about 3 minutes, and then turn them and fry the bottom side just until it begins to color, about 1 minute longer.

5. Arrange the muffins on the greased cookie sheet. Carefully break 1 egg into each "well." Season with pepper to taste and cover each egg with a slice of the heated ham or bacon. Bake for 5 minutes, or just until the eggs set and the ham is slightly browned and begins to curl at the edges.

6. Place each egg on an individual serving plate, spoon 2 table-spoons of sauce over the top, and serve with any remaining sauce in a sauceboat on the side.

NOTE: If the sauce is prepared in advance, add a little beef broth or white wine when you reheat it to prevent thickening.

8.

BASICS

MAYONNAISE
SALSA MAHONESA

MAKES 2 CUPS

2 egg yolks
1½ tablespoons white wine vinegar
½ teaspoon salt, or to taste
¼ teaspoon freshly ground white pepper, or to taste
2 cups olive or vegetable oil
2 tablespoons boiling water or broth (beef or vegetable)

1. Place the egg yolks, vinegar, salt, and white pepper in a bowl. Mix together with a whisk. The ingredients can also be combined in a blender.

2. Add the oil in a slow, steady drizzle, whisking constantly until emulsified. Whisk in the boiling water or broth, and correct the seasonings to taste. The mayonnaise should be refrigerated if not to be used within a few minutes.

VARIATION: To make Mustard Sauce, add 2 teaspoons Dijon mustard to 1 cup mayonnaise; mix well.

172

TOMATO SAUCE
SALSA DE TOMATE

MAKES 3 TO 4 CUPS

3 tablespoons olive or vegetable oil
1 clove garlic
2 ounces cooked ham, diced
1 heaping tablespoon finely diced onion
1 bay leaf, crumbled
pinch dried thyme
2 to 3 parsley stems, chopped
1 teaspoon paprika
1 pound plum tomatoes, peeled, seeded, and chopped
salt to taste
pinch sugar
⅓ cup beef broth
12-inch piece celery

1. Heat the oil in a large saucepan. Add the garlic, and sauté until golden. Add the ham, and stir to combine. Add the onion, bay leaf, thyme, and parsley stems, and sauté until the onion is transparent, but not browned. Stir in the paprika. Add the tomatoes, season with the salt and sugar, and simmer over moderate heat for 10 minutes, stirring occasionally.

2. Stir in the beef broth and the celery, and cook, stirring occasionally, for 10 minutes longer. Remove from heat, and strain the sauce through a colander, pressing to force the sauce through. Correct seasonings, and serve.

ARAGON SAUCE
SALSA ARAGONESA

MAKES 1 CUP

1 teaspoon freshly squeezed lemon juice
1 tablespoon cold water
2 egg yolks
⅔ cup fine-quality olive oil

1. Place the lemon juice, water, and egg yolks in a copper or Pyrex saucepan or casserole. Place over medium heat, and whisk until the mixture is smooth and creamy. Remove from heat, and let cool slightly.

2. Add the oil in a slow, steady drizzle, whisking constantly until emulsified. Pour the sauce through a sieve. Use as desired.

NOTE: Once half the oil is added, if the sauce seems too thick, whisk in 1 to 2 teaspoons cold water, then the remaining oil. This sauce can also be thickened by combining with a white sauce made with ¾ tablespoon butter, 1 heaping tablespoon flour, and 1 cup milk, and cooked for 5 minutes, whisking constantly, until creamy.

CREAMY MUSTARD SAUCE

Delicious with cold meats and cold cuts.

MAKES ¾ TO 1 CUP

2 teaspoons mustard
1 teaspoon freshly squeezed lemon juice
freshly ground white pepper to taste
½ cup heavy cream, well chilled

Place the mustard, lemon juice, and white pepper in a small bowl, and whisk together. Whisk in the heavy cream in a slow, steady drizzle until the sauce is emulsified. Chill until ready to serve.

LIGHT BÉCHAMEL SAUCE
SALSA BÉCHAMEL (Clara)

MAKES ABOUT 2 CUPS

4 tablespoons butter
¼ cup all-purpose flour
2 cups scalded milk
salt and freshly ground white pepper to taste
pinch grated nutmeg

1. Melt the butter in a saucepan. Add the flour, and stir to form a smooth paste. Slowly whisk in the scalded milk, blending well to prevent lumps from forming. Cook over medium heat for 5 minutes, whisking constantly, until a smooth, creamy sauce is formed.

2. Remove from heat, and season with the salt, pepper, and nutmeg.

A RICHER BÉCHAMEL
SALSA BÉCHAMEL (Espesa)

MAKES ABOUT 2 CUPS

5½ tablespoons butter
⅓ cup all-purpose flour
2 cups scalded milk
salt and freshly ground white pepper to taste
pinch grated nutmeg

1. Melt the butter in a saucepan. Add the flour, and stir to form a smooth paste. Slowly whisk in the hot milk, blending well to prevent lumps from forming. Cook over medium heat for 5 minutes, whisking constantly, until a smooth creamy sauce is formed.

2. Remove from heat, and season with salt, pepper, and nutmeg.

FISH BATTER
MASA DE FREIR CON LEVADURA SARRAU

Use as needed to coat fish or shellfish for frying. This can also be used to fry squid.

2 cups all-purpose flour
2 teaspoons dry yeast
1 cup lukewarm milk
½ teaspoon salt
¼ teaspoon freshly ground black pepper
pinch grated nutmeg
3 tablespoons olive oil, heated and cooled

Place the flour and yeast in a large mixing bowl, and blend well. Make a well in the center. Add ⅔ cup milk, and the remaining ingredients. Mix well with your hands or in a mixer with a dough hook attachment, adding the remaining milk gradually, until a smooth dough is formed.

BEER-FLAVORED FISH BATTER
MASA PARA PESCADO FRITO

Dredge pieces of fish (or squid) in flour before coating in this batter to fry.

¾ cup all-purpose flour
1 tablespoon olive oil
1 egg, slightly beaten
½ teaspoon salt
pinch freshly ground black pepper
2 tablespoons cold water
⅓ cup beer

1. Place the flour in a mixing bowl, and form a well in the center. To the well, add the oil, egg, salt, pepper, and water, and mix well. Add half of the beer, and beat well with an electric mixer until the batter is smooth. Add the remaining beer, and mix 30 seconds longer to blend. Press the batter through a colander into a bowl.

2. Let rest for 1 hour before using to coat fish for frying.

VINAIGRETTE A

Generally served with asparagus, artichokes, and other green vegetables.

MAKES ABOUT ½ CUP

3 tablespoons white wine vinegar
½ teaspoon salt
¼ teaspoon freshly ground white pepper
⅓ cup olive oil

In a small bowl combine the vinegar, salt, and pepper. Moments before serving, drizzle in the oil, whisking constantly, until the ingredients are emulsified.

VINAIGRETTE B

A special sauce for fish.

MAKES ABOUT 1 CUP

1 heaping tablespoon finely chopped onion
1 dark green lettuce leaf, finely chopped
1 egg, hard-boiled, chopped
½ clove garlic, minced
1 tablespoon chopped pickle
3 tablespoons white wine vinegar
⅓ cup cold water
salt and freshly ground white pepper to taste
⅓ cup olive oil

In a bowl combine all the ingredients except the oil. Then add the oil in a slow steady drizzle until the ingredients are emulsified.

VINAIGRETTE C

For cold cooked meats.

MAKES ABOUT 2½ CUPS

Prepare as for Vinaigrette B, above, adding ½ pound seeded diced tomatoes, and 1 to 2 chopped, roasted sweet red peppers (page 183) along with the other vegetables.

GLOSSARY

Certain simple ingredients, utensils, and cooking techniques are key to the art of Spanish cooking, and to translating Spanish cooking to the North American kitchen. (Top-quality olive oil, garlic, saffron, and fresh spices are used in even the simplest of tapas recipes, for example.) The basic descriptions that follow include those that you will need to enjoy the tapas in this book. Although the majority of the ingredients and utensils are available in supermarkets, specialty stores, and cookware departments of this country, American substitutes are given for those that may still prove elusive, and for those cooks who prefer to use equivalents they may already have at home.

CHEESES

Burgos: Burgos cheese comes in the form of a curved loaf of bread. Soft Burgos cheese will keep its freshness for up to 10 days or so; hard Burgos cheese will keep well for more than a year, during which it acquires an even better taste and consistency. Serve Burgos cheese in slices or cubes.

Burriana: This cheese from eastern Spain is sold fresh and is a favorite in Valencia.

Cabrales: Queso de Cabrales is quite similar to Roquefort and, according to some of the finest palates, is often preferred to Roquefort. A well-known cheese from the town in Asturias for which it is named, Cabrales boasts an exquisite, smooth flavor, subtle spiciness, and buttery texture. It is a true delicacy.

Castillblanco: This cheese is made from the first of March to the first of September. It is made from the milk of the goat, and lamb, depending on the part of Spain from which it comes. Castillblanco cheeses are small, and are generally eaten 8 to 10 days after they are prepared. They are served in abundance in the *colmados* of Seville.

C.R.A.M.T.: This cheese is quite similar to Cabrales cheese, although even richer, and most definitely superior to Roquefort.

Gabas: Gabas is a goat cheese and is prepared in the northeastern province of Huesca. Gabas is made in small salted jars. A delicious appetizer, Gabas cheese should be served in thin slices with toasted bread.

Mahón: Surprisingly, this exquisite cheese is not well-known. It is made from goat's milk, which is, on exception, mixed with cow's milk. Mahón cheese is aged for 1 year. To serve, cut the cheese into small cubes or thin slices. It is a superb appetizer, especially when served with sherry.

Manchego: Manchego cheese, although difficult to come by in the United States, is worth the search. Made from sheep's milk, Manchego is renowned, especially in central Spain. It is delicious fresh, and when preserved in a bath of vinegar, Manchego acquires an excellent, savory, and rich taste—a perfect tapa to be doused with a sweet manzanilla or aromatic Oloroso sherry.

Roncal: Delicate-tasting Roncal cheese, made in the Pyrenees, is widely enjoyed throughout Aragon and the Basque provinces. It is juicy, although quite dense on the inside, and its rind is hard. The small and round Roncal cheeses are made from sheep's milk and, in rare cases, cow's milk. Serve Roncal in thin slices.

Villalon: Villalon cheese is eaten fresh and salted. A favorite throughout Madrid and Castile, Villalon is made from sheep's milk in the town of Villalon in the province of Valladolid. It is a good cheese, fresh as well as salted, and an especially savory tapa.

FISH AND SHELLFISH

The freshness and variety of seafood tapas in Spain is unsurpassed. To recreate these delectable treats at home, use only the freshest fish and shellfish. The tips below will help you in the selection and preparation of seafood for the recipes in this book.

Clams: Fresh littleneck clams work best for the tapas recipes in this book. Pick through the clams carefully and discard any that are open or have broken shells. Scrub the clams well and place them in a pot with salted cold water to cover. Add 1 tablespoon cornmeal per gallon of water to help release sand or grit. Let soak for 3 to 12 hours. Rinse and drain well before cooking.

Dried Salt Codfish: Dried salt codfish, a favorite for tapas recipes, must be soaked in cold water before cooking to remove salt. Place the cod in a large pot or bowl with cold water to cover. Soak at room temperature for at least 24 hours, changing the water frequently. Rinse and drain well before cooking.

Eel: To clean eel, make an incision in the skin of the eel about a thumb's length below the tip of the head and slit the skin all the way around. Grip or anchor the head securely, and pull the skin below the incision down until it is completely removed from the body. Slit the underbelly of the eel and pull out the entrails. Rinse well.

Fish Broth: A basic ingredient for many tapas recipes, fish broth is quite easy to prepare at home. Combine 2 fresh fish heads, 1 leek, and 1 bouquet garni in a saucepan. Add 1 quart water and bring to a boil. Simmer for 10 minutes, or until the liquid is reduced by almost half. Remove from heat. Strain the broth, and use as desired. Makes about 2 cups.

Mussels: Choose mussels carefully, and discard any with open or broken shells. Scrub the mussels well to remove sand and dirt, scrape off any barnacles adhered to the shells with a knife, and remove the beards. Place the mussels in a pot with salted cold water to cover. Add 1 tablespoon cornmeal or flour per gallon of water and let the mussels soak for 1 to 2 hours. This step helps rid the mussels of any dirt or grit inside the shells and is particularly important for recipes that require the mussels to remain in the shell when added to a sauce. Drain the mussels well and proceed to cook as required.

Octopus: Octopus are simple to clean. First, cut out the eyes and discard. Then pull up the hood of the head and rinse well. Pull the hood back down. The octopus is now ready to cook. Once cooked, grip the purple membrane from one edge of the head and pull off. Repeat for the tentacles.

Sardines: Nothing quite parallels fresh sardines in bringing to any table a true flavor of the Mediterranean. In choosing fresh sardines, be sure that the eyes are clear and that the sardines have a "fishy" smell but no foul odor. Often times, sardines sold as fresh in this country have been sitting on ice for some time and may not be worth purchasing. To clean sardines, first cut off the heads and discard. Scrape off the scales and remove the fins with a knife. Make a slit across the length of the belly of the fish to the tail and remove the guts. Rinse well, and pat dry.

Snails: Choose large white snails. Rub the shells with coarse salt and white wine vinegar. Place the snails in a large pot and rinse in several changes of cold water. Drain well, and fill the pot once more with cold water to cover the snails. Cover and let soak for about 4 hours, changing the water several times. Rinse well, drain, and cook as desired.

Squid: Choose squid which are pinkish white or light purple in color. Do not use any squid that have blackened flesh or a bad odor other than a normal fishy smell. To clean the squid, grip the body of the squid with one hand, and pull off the head and tentacles with the other hand. Cut the tentacles from the head. Remove the ink sac and save it if to be used for color and flavoring. Discard the head. Remove the cartilage attached to the tentacles and the clear, flat bone inside the body. Pull the thin membranelike skin off the body of the squid and discard the skin. Cut the body and tentacles as required in the recipe.

Marinated Tuna: Spain's version of tuna in a can is called *atun en escabeche*, or literally "marinated tuna." It is simply poached tuna packed in a dressing of vinegar, peppercorns, and onion. To prepare your own version at home, add 1 tablespoon white wine vinegar, 2 to 3 black peppercorns, and half a small onion, sliced, to one 6½-ounce can of white albacore tuna, drained. Let marinate 24 hours to add a tangy flavor to plain tuna. (Plain drained tuna can be used as a substitute for the Spanish version for those who prefer a less pronounced taste.)

HERBS, SPICES, AND OILS

Although relatively few spices, herbs, and varieties of oils are used in Spanish cooking, some are basic to Spanish cooking in general and would be dearly missed if omitted.

Olive Oil: Superior-quality olive oil is perhaps the most important ingredient in Spanish cooking, as well as in Mediterranean cooking in general. Many varieties of olive oil are available today, from a deep green to a clear golden color, varying in taste and purity. Today, quite fortunately for lovers of Spanish cuisine, olive oil is replacing other commonly used oils because of its low level of polyunsaturated fats. All olive oils have varying degrees of acidity. When using olive oil for frying, a quick way to rid the oil of any acidlike taste is to heat it in a skillet to the smoking point, then add a few sprigs of parsley to fry. Remove the parsley, strain the oil in a very fine sieve, and it is ready to use. Vegetable oil or a combination of olive and vegetable oil can be used for frying for those who prefer a more subtle tasting oil than pure olive oil. To give olive oil a garlicky flavor, Spaniards sauté a whole clove of garlic in the oil until it is golden, then discard the garlic before going on with the recipe. Tried and true, this simple technique is a mainstay in learning how to give food a Spanish flair.

Paprika: Paprika, a powdered spice made from the ground pods of sweet peppers, is frequently used in tapas recipes. In Spain, two varieties, hot and sweet, are available. Both can be found in specialty shops in this country and should be used whenever possible as indicated.

Picadas: To flavor foods and give added texture to sauces, Spanish cooking employs *picadas*—finely ground pastes of spices, seasonings, and toasted ground nuts. Often consisting of readily available ingredients such as garlic, parsley, and almonds, picadas can be prepared the traditional way with a mortar and pestle, or in a blender or food processor in large quantities.

Ramo de hierbas: A *ramo de hierbas* (literally "bunch of herbs") or bouquet garni, the more commonly used culinary term, is used to add flavor to the soup stocks or stews used in many tapas recipes. The *ramo* can be prepared by using 2 small stalks of celery as a splint to hold a few sprigs of parsley, 1 bay leaf, and fresh thyme, if available. Commercially prepared bouquet garni in bottles can also be used; however, fresh ingredients will give the fuller flavor.

Saffron: The dried burnt-red stigma of a purple crocus, saffron lends both color and taste to a multitude of dishes in Spanish cooking. Saffron is sold in tiny vials or packets in most specialty shops and some grocery stores. It is available in strands or as a powder. Originally used for medicinal purposes and as a dye, saffron is used in very small quantities for cooking. A few strands of the stigma or a pinch of the powder will do. Because of the distinct pungent taste saffron lends to any dish, substitutes which simply add the yellow color to foods—for example, turmeric or yellow food coloring—should never be used as a substitute in recipes requiring saffron.

OLIVES

Olives, Black: Toss black olives with this Spanish marinade for a delightful, simple tapa: 1 medium onion, thinly sliced, 3 cloves garlic mashed together with ¼ cup finely chopped parsley, 3 tablespoons white vinegar, ¼ cup good quality olive oil, and salt to taste.

Olives, Green: In Spain, Sevillian olives are sold in glass jars or wooden barrels of various shapes and sizes. They are often stuffed, usually with strips of red pimento or anchovies. They come in different sizes and types, but the best are the Sevillian and Manzanillian varieties. Here in the United States, a few slices of lemon and orange together with a few tiny new potatoes added to the marinade in which green olives are packed prevent them from discoloring and add flavor.

PEPPERS

Roasted Sweet Peppers (Pimentos): To prepare pimentos at home, choose large unblemished sweet red peppers. Place the peppers on the broiler rack about 6 inches below the flame. Broil the peppers until the skin is charred (but not burned) and blistered all over, turning frequently to cook evenly all around. Remove from heat, and place the peppers in a paper bag. Set aside until cool enough to handle. Carefully peel the skin off the cooled peppers, remove stems and seeds, and use as desired. (The peppers will keep in a covered container in the refrigerator for several days.)

SAUSAGES AND CURED HAM

Spanish sausages and cured ham, among the most delicious of tapas and the easiest to serve, require some special introduction. Spicy, flavorful, and almost addictive, they can be served in a variety of attractive ways, all of them savory. Whether sliced thin and perched atop slices of crusty bread, or roasted and skewered, at least a few selections of the numerous Spanish sausage varieties make a tapas bar complete. Most are available in specialty shops in the United States. A few of Spain's favorite and best-known sausages and Spain's favorite Serrano ham are listed below.

Butifarra Sausage:

Chorizo: One of the most common and best known of Spanish sausages, chorizo, a cured pork sausage, is delicious plain, roasted, in rice dishes, stews, or on pastry. Chorizo is quite readily available in many specialty shops. In a bind, Italian pepperoni, which does have a slightly different flavor and is usually wider than chorizo, can be substituted.

Longaniza: A thin sausage made with spiced ground pork, longaniza sausage is available in Spanish or Latin American specialty shops. Use any favorite fine-quality pork sausage as a substitute.

Morcilla: Sometimes called blood sausage or black pudding, morcilla is used throughout Spain and Latin America in stews, thick soups, or roasted as the center of a main meal. Made from cooked pork blood, it is quite spicy and some varieties include finely chopped onion.

Serrano Ham: A cured ham used in many tapas recipes and other Spanish dishes, Serrano ham is delicious served very thinly sliced upon tiny crusty rolls. Spanish Serrano ham can be found in specialty shops; if not, fine-quality Italian prosciutto can be substituted.

Sobrasada: A specialty from the island of Majorca off the Iberian Peninsula, sobrasada is a cured sausage and is perfect for a fast and easy tapa. Sobrasada is available in specialty shops. A fine substitute is the more common Italian sopprasata variety.

WINES AND SHERRIES

Cariñena: A very sweet and aromatic red wine named for the city of Cariñena in the province of Zaragoza.

Manzanilla: A white dry sherry made in Sanlúcar de Barrameda and other places in the province of Andalusia.

Priorato: Red wine from the Catalan *comarca* of Priorato.

Valdepeñas: Red wine from Valdepeñas, a town in the province of Ciudad Real.

COOKWARE

Cazuelas de barro: These shallow adobe-colored casseroles, either clay or earthenware, are very common in Spain and are especially appropriate for preparing and serving tapas, because they convert easily from cooking to serving dishes and retain heat or cold. *Cazuelas* are available in various sizes, and can be found in specialty shops in this country. Oven to table-top glass cookware does nicely in its place.

Paellera: Named for paella, the renowned dish for which it was designed, this wide, shallow, round skilletlike pan with two handles on either side is usually made of steel. It is ideal for holding the large quantities of rice, seafood, and chicken for which paella is famous worldwide, and is in general the preferred vessel for rice-based tapas. A large shallow skillet is a good substitute for the paellera, although, like the cazuela de barro, it is available in North American specialty shops and through catalogues.

Index